WEALTH CREATION

THE CREDIT SCORE

Your Credit Score is one of the most paralyzing numbers you will ever face.

Rob Wilson

(Wealth Creation - The Credit Score)

ISBN 978-0-9721065-5-9

Printed in USA

Dedication

These series of Wealth Creation is dedicated to the many families that I have comes across in my work. It is also dedicated to you the now reader, whether you are reading just this book or the entire series, I am in prayer that you experience wealth creation personally.

I especially wish that you who have chosen to read this series find what they are seeking.

To:

____

Rob Wilson

N
U
M
B
E
R
?

A CREDIT SCORE is a three digit number design to illustrate your borrowing risk.

Table of Contents

Foreword

It is my honor to write this Forward on behalf of Rob Wilson regarding his latest work related to wealth creation. The number of people negatively affected by their credit scores is astounding.

In this work, Rob gives insight to readers who have never been taught that their credit and credit scores are directly related to their level of mastery of managing money.

As a former employee of 2 different credit reporting agencies, Rob Wilson understands that a consumer's credit profile and credit scores mirror how they manage their money.

The importance of credit in our society has created the proliferation of credit repair/restoration organizations to "help" individuals who have not properly managed their money.

This entire series on wealth creation that Mr. Wilson has put together is truly designed to take an individual through the process of "reorganizing" their mindset and their finances to accomplish a greater personal goal.

By: C.W. Copeland, Ph.D., ChFC®, CLU®, RICP®

Preface

Since 2001 I have carried the name The Credit Surgeon, it all happened when I first started teaching credit and credit scores on radio across America. In many ways I hated the name and the box that it put me in. Your credit score is big than a trade line, its more than just credit, it is a measurement of who you are or supposed to be.

I teach many of classes on money management and debt management along with wealth creation. Never is credit mentioned as a part of the process, never do I teach about interest rate and most of the stuff that you have been learning.

I want to be quick to say this because I do not wish to offend many of my colleagues in this space. Much of the information that you have been taught may be misleading or incorrect. However, much of it is capable of getting you through the back door.

There is so much in this space that I believe hurt minorities more than any other group of people. Let look at a couple of things right off the top. If the is to improve and build credit scores over 750 (which is the beginning of good credit) why are they so many consumer finance companies in your community?

How do banks earn 100's of millions of dollars on fees alone? Why are there rent to own furniture and appliances companies in the heart of the community. Why would a payday lender or title loan company be in areas where banks use to be?

If for no other reason than you caring enough about changing your process with how you want the financial system to view and respect you, prepare yourself for a new journey. As I am writing this there is a debate in my head, should I put this on paper?

Unlike most of the people who have learned credit information from several type of entities and not directly from the source. I have worked with and worked designing scoring models with two different credit reporting services. I know a lot more than many who's information I may seem to be attacking.

If you are reading this book I believe that you are of a different mindset and if you are you will benefit from this greatly. If by chance you are reading this book before you have read Wealth Creation "The Mindset and The Influencer" it's okay. Normally I would want you to read those first. But if you have already read those books this will simply be a nice blend of knowledge.

You need to know and understanding how credit works can help you improve your credit score. I know that credit is taught as that one piece in which it opens the door to better interest rates, rewards credit cards or even a mortgage. Did you know that 87% of minorities buy a home with bad credit and it is promoted as a good rate? Any home purchased with a score under 750 is bad credit. Fact!

With all of the misleading and incorrect information about credit floating around, it's no wonder some people feel lost when it comes to your credit reports and credit scores. Most people do not know the difference between credit, a credit score and a credit report—but I will set everything straight with simple and clear explanations.

I am going to take the time to compile the most important credit facts you need to know to understand your credit, your credit score and credit report and everything that impacts it. Most importantly, I will set many of the records straight when it comes to credit myths that have been lingering for too long.

Introduction

Wealth Creation "The Credit Score", I am going to attempt to put most of everything I know about the credit score. I will also try to drive home a lot of different points to ensure that you can apply the information in this book to your life.

First thing, you need to have true basic knowledge about this billion dollar industry. Everything you will need to achieve your credit score goals is really simple. You should know that there are 3-bureau credit report from Experian, Equifax and TransUnion

These 3 agencies collect and report data regarding your personal credit trades (accounts) and/ or transactions that is monitored for changes alerts, updates, and alert triggers, timing and frequencies vary by credit bureau.

They even offer a form of protection with some benefits for identity theft. It is an insurance that is underwritten and administered by American Bankers Insurance Company of Florida, an Assurant company.

You will see me refer to the FICO® scores most of the time because 90% of lenders use FICO® scores. You can get your score from other sources but keep in mind that other scores can be off by up to 100 points – if not more.

It’s also important that you get your credit report from all three bureaus (www.annualcreditreport.com) it is easy to instantly access your credit report from Experian, Equifax, and TransUnion. This is where you check for errors and get a complete look at your credit standing in a glance.

Being able to see what's affecting your score really takes the mystery out of why your credit score is what it is. You will see the top factors that are determining your FICO Score along with detailed content. Some of them have gotten so smart that you can use a simulator to helps you explore potential impacts of your decisions on your credit before you make them.

An insight has never hurt anyone, the credit score versions that lenders actually use sometimes is a different versions of the FICO Score for different purposes. You should want your lender to get the versions most frequently used for mortgage, auto and credit card lending. So, no matter your credit goals, you should want to have access to the most widely-used FICO Scores.

The Credit Score

Chapter One

Control Your Money!

Earlier I stated how I do not primarily teach about credit or interest rate. Why? Let's start by looking at anything that may be negative, it is often connected to things that bring or cause pressure. Things that are challenging that bring discouragement.

I can work with you about bad debt, charged off accounts, even collection agencies, but that is operating in the negative. Credit is for poor people. Let that sink in for a few minutes (I repeat, credit is for poor people), if you really think about it you will agree.

Follow me for a minute, look at what I am saying by class.

Class 1 – Poverty – limited financial resources make it difficult for parents to maintain a work-life balance that allows them to spend time at home caring for their children and to be active and involved with school, extracurricular activities, and community life.

Now, consider what type of financial tools they have at their disposal? Look at their community and review all of the financial resources available to them. Payday lenders, no credit check lending based on television, cars, furniture and jewelry used as collateral. No co-signer here.

What is not known here by those who live in poverty is their ability to work their way out. The fact that any form of income that exists can become or should I say creates a pathway out. It's unlikely to happen because of the opportunity cost to make such a change.

Class 2 – Low Income – Families with low to moderate-income face many challenges. You know they are a step above Class 1, even though there could be more money and resources they can experience the difficulty to feed, clothe, or shelter family members. However, there are different sets of groups and organizations that help low income families and meet their fundamental needs.

Don't get me wrong here, in life, there are times when you need assistance. While adults are proud of their independence, there are times when they need assistance. When they admit they can't do it independently, they may feel weak. There may also be a fear of stigmas associated with people who need assistance. The truth is, we all need help at one point or another.

Here credit is available under certain conditions like higher interest rate, large payment requirements, payday lending, title loans, rent to own and co-signers. Credit is always available to you, it is the cost that you will pay for credit.

Class 3 – Working – I was born and raised poor. I always believed that the working class was people who do manual labor for a living. This can mean anyone in a job like a janitor, plumber or beat cop walking the street. If someone would be considered blue collar, if they don't sit in an office or work mostly at a computer, if they can wear jeans and a t-shirt instead of a suit and tie into work, they are probably part of the traditional working class.

Working class used to be about the kind of job you had. Today it's more a description of economic uncertainty. People in the working class work and know that they have to keep working in a way that the middle class never will.

The working class has generally fallen out of favor. In part this is because it is seen as an insult. Being a member of the working class was to be crude and have lower status than a white collar (Middle) worker. This is both an inappropriate way to discuss anyone and, frankly, inaccurate.

Credit here is far greater than the previous classes, yet it operates in a place very close to bad credit as it relates to score. This group generally cannot afford financial hardship. They rarely are able to meet the average daily balance minimum with their bank. They can only afford to pay the minimum payment on their credit card balances.

Class 4 – Middle – It's funny how economists and politicians often use the terms "working class" and "middle class" and they do so very casually but carelessly. There are many articles on income, labor and policy but no one ever seems to slow down long enough to clarify what either status actually means. So let me do my little part to continue to make my point.

Remember, I am showing class in order to establish that credit is now targeted for poor people/low to moderate income.

This middle class group is attached to anyone who makes a certain amount of money compared to the rest of us. There is a standard that most middle class is defined by how much you make compared to the median income where you live.

Credit here is easy, scores are maintained merely because these people make enough money that they really never experience financial hardship. They carry bank account balances well beyond the average daily minimum, they payoff credit card charges each month. (What's in your wallet?) LOL

What I want you to learn here about credit more than anything else is that everyone can get credit regardless of their score or income class. The difference between what is going on here is what you pay for that credit. I know anytime I try to talk about edgy stuff like this I have a brain freeze on what I should write. I am trying to push through.

Most of you will agree that much of the "working class" has come to fill in the bottom section of the middle class as it relates to income. Their positioning is below that of what is associated with the middle class but above that which is associated with the "lower class."

More people fall into the lower-middle zone I discussed above. They make more than the poverty line, and may even technically make enough to be earning a middle class income, but they still live paycheck to paycheck.

The working class today describes having a job but feeling poor, or making enough to get by without much else. This is not a description of poverty or unemployment, but neither is it the description of comfort. When you associate credit to all of this madness you should understand there is a task navigating credit scores.

According to Investopedia.com, there are five main income classes. I want you to read these and factor in what you are learning and what you know about credit. Can you begin to see the margin, the process of this thing called CREDIT?

1) The Upper class

The "upper class" basically means the upper 1% of America. To gain a place in this income class, you need to earn at least $389,436 a year. On average, the upper 1% earns $1.2 million each year.

2) The Upper-Middle class

According to the Census Bureau, 6.1% of households earn $200,000 or more and 14.1% bring in $100,000 to $200,000 a year. This is the upper middle class.

3) The Middle-Middle class

The great majority of people land here, with an income of between $35,000 to $100,000. Of everyone in the United States, 41.5% can honestly say that they are part of the middle-class.

4) The Lower-Middle class

This class earns between $18,871 and $47,100. They straddle the lower-line of poverty and the upper edge of the middle middle class. They're not technically poor, but they're dang close…

5) The Poverty Level

The lowest income class is those that don't earn enough to meet their basic needs (food, shelter, and clothing). Earning less than $18,871 is an unbelievable 14% of the U.S.

Credit is a bartering service concept that got out of hand, meaning it started shifting from need to wants. Once it arrived in the want category it became a need to evaluate the risk associated to the extension of goods and a cost.

People get the two (credit and credit scores) confused. I cannot tell you the number of time that I get into discussions about how people with low scores (very low) can still get credit. Some of you that might read this book will relate to my next statement.

Client files bankruptcy chapter 7, not long after going out and purchasing a brand new car. They wrote me this long email about how I was wrong about the impact of their decision to file. Here is just a part of it.

"Mr. Wilson, we are amazed by the fact that people actually pay you for the direction of their financial lives. We probably should request a refund from you, but we will not. We will start teaching people what we learned in the last five months.

Also, your advice to not file bankruptcy is crazy, instead of paying settlement on old credit cards, we paid nothing. You said credit would be hard if we filed and that is not sure. There are credit card offers already coming in the mail.

We signed a new lease for our apartment and we only have rent and the car payment. The bankruptcy was much easier than we thought. So, we are going to work our way back and rebuild our credit, we are already doing that, but will add more. You should learn from this and the advice that you give."

I wanted so badly to call them and give them some choice words, but I did not, I actually am speaking of it for the first time. There is a lot to process here, first this family only had two credit cards in delinquency and charged off. There were three others which were at roughly 50% of the available limits.

A few medical bills and small loans were very manageable. One of the delinquent credit cards was threatening to file a lawsuit for payment. All in all this is manageable, you have options and you can maintain a credit score and protect you financial future.

But, you must understand what is going on here totally and the impact of your decision (the opportunity cost) that will affect your results. By negotiating the two charged off cards and reaching a settlement they would have paid less out of pocket money. Yes the charged off accounts are hurting their score and the unpaid balance as well, but the damage is done.

The medical bills and small loans would be next to deal with and eliminate while working to get the other credit cards under 30% (I will share why later) of the credit limit. The result of all of this would preserve what they have already established even with the bad credit.

If they would have stayed with this process, their personal credit score would have improved dramatically in less than six months. They would have remained intact and capable of purchasing a home now, not a new lease. The same money used to file bankruptcy and purchase the car would have given them better results.

I know, I know…

Some of you are saying they will get a fresh start. THERE IS NO FRESH START….

One of the toughest things I have to do as an educator in this financial space is to debunk much of the misinformation or incomplete information you receive. Yes, they call it a fresh start after you have discharged all of your unsecured debt. The fact is the bankruptcy comes with its own damage, like you will be able to purchase a home for two years. All of your basic services including your car insurance and rental insurance will be impacted, employment and health insurance will be impacted as well.

The stigma behind the bankruptcy will transfer to the purchase of a new or old car. Yes you will receive credit cards and each of them will carry high interest rates. The consumer loans will carry an unforgiving rate all because of the bankruptcy itself.

Do not get me wrong here, there is life after bankruptcy and it can be what you make it. You get a chance to make some new choices and to strip some sources of stress from your life. Your damaged credit improves over time, just like wounds heal. You still have work to do after your bankruptcy to enjoy your fresh start. Figure out where you are, money wise, and apply the lessons of your past and any financial education class you may have to take to get the discharge.

Money management is the key!

For people who are struggling with credit card debt and have a low credit score, money management is what will help you rebuild credit and contribute to improving your credit score over time. While there is no immediate way to get a higher credit score, I have found that money management is the key that will give you total improvement, you will see continuous gains as your payment history improves and your credit utilization goes down.

Most of the people who are facing some kind of financial challenge may be behind on their mortgage, overwhelmed by student loan debt, or struggling to fund their retirement. The majority, however, are trying to manage more debt without managing their money.

I know you are interested in increasing your credit score as well as wealth creation. Here is a big secret that I am trying to help you discover. Money management and wealth creation will get you where you want to be.

It can be very difficult to learn to manage money. However, if you ever want to transition from simply "having money" to "wealthy," you need to understand the importance of money management and begin implementing it in regards to your finances. CONTROL YOUR MONEY! (CYM)

Those who make a decent amount of money but aren't practicing money management tend to simply spend money without any rhyme, reason, or purpose. Money comes in and it goes out, while the person remains stagnant and doesn't ever move forward. You just read about the various financial classes.

On the other hand, those who have wealth tend to have peace of mind. They aren't looking for money or things for fulfillment, yet they know that they have all that they need and will continue to throughout their life. They do not focus on getting a high score, their focus is wealth creation.

To embrace money management is to learn financial practices that help you accumulate wealth and security, while understanding the key to preserving that wealth. Implementing the management of your money (CYM) takes your unique needs, goals, and risks into consideration while focusing on your financial decision making and your previous habits that could stand in the way of your success. It also includes a humble awareness of certain factors outside of your control, such as inflation, taxes, debt, and the market volatility as we are experiencing in 2022.

Learning the basic tenets of money management will help you to understand why it's important and how to start implementing the practice for yourself. By not understanding the foundation of money creates a multitude of issues. For example, if you aren't aware of the way credit and interest works, you might charge something small on a credit card that ends up costing you 20 percent or more in interest over the course of a year.

In fact, you could end up paying for that one thing over and over again, essentially throwing your money away, and making it difficult to achieve a higher credit score. I mention this because far too often when I talk with groups and wealth creation they ask more questions about credit and when I talk about credit scores they have no questions about wealth creation.

Without a firm, educated grasp of financial matters and how this system really works, you'll likely end up like the majority of people; locked into years of debt, paying high fees, and unsure where all of your money is going.

Money management and wealth creation is all about accumulation. Many people don't understand this. They view wealth as making a lot of money and don't realize that if they're spending that money, no matter how much it is, and not accumulating it, they're never going to be wealthy. It's likely that their credit score is suffering because of.

This is why you need a way to determine where your money is going. The best way to do this is to control your money (CYM) to see where you're spending it. When you are able to see where your money is going, you will then be able to develop a strategic spending plan for using, saving and investing it more effectively.

I say this everywhere I go, everybody you do business with understands the importance of money management in business and focuses on increasing their monthly profits. However, increasing profit isn't the end goal.

Using the increased profit wisely to further financial growth is essential. Thus, creating a money management plan that includes investment of the additional profit will increase the wealth of the business exponentially. For example, taking advantage of planning for retirement, and understanding how much you should be putting into an investment is a great step to take to get better control of your money.

It does not matter whether you are managing money for yourself or your business, the stronger your money management plan, and the more control you have over the flow of your cash, the closer you are to reaching your (get this will you) credit, credit score and wealth creation goals.

Later I will be talking about the factors that your scores are based on, there are five key factors that most lenders use to make their lending decisions. As I go over each of them, ask yourself how this relates to my money management and wealth creation goals.

This will be a huge transformation point for you if you connect the dots. Do not try to compare this to other people or things that you know of, make this all about you as it should be. Your finances are your finger print and your credit is personal don't play games that you do not understand all of the rules. I am going to try and expose to you the rules.

Chapter Two

The Credit Report

Let me start-off by saying what you already know about credit. Without it (good credit), your financial life will struggle. Even though you may have the ability to get credit, it ends up costing you the highest interest rate.

Credit impact every household is some form. With the latest fallout of the financial industry there was a huge credit crunch. All across the financial industry lenders have started tightening their standards across the board, raising the minimum requirements for their lowest-interest loans, declining loans in sharply unstable housing markets, and capping the amount they are willing to loan a borrower.

Credit card companies and banks are reducing lines of credit in which they had previously offered to consumers. Insurance companies (Home, Car, Life and Health) even tightened their standards.

What I hope to do in this book is provide you a new and different approach to understanding credit and credit scores. The goal is to show how it works and most importantly how you should work with credit.

Understand that credit scores are used by the vast majority of lenders, banks and insurance companies to measure your credit and insurance risk. It's in your best interest to know how to improve your scores in order to improve your chances of getting approved at the best rates with the best terms. In this book you'll learn the basics of how scoring models work and how to maximize your scores.

The Report

I want to take this time to provide you with information that most should already know. This information is about your credit report and what you will find on it. Later on, you will be able to connect the dots with other information, which should give you a better understanding of how the current system works.

I have identified eleven sections on your report, which I hope to familiarize you with and give you a clearer picture as to how you can increase and change your score over time. If you do not have a copy of your credit report, please visit www.annualcreditreport.com. You are entitled under federal law to receive at least one free from all three credit reporting agencies.

Let's get started looking at some basic things that confuse a lot of people. At the very top right of the report is The Heading. It contains the Credit Bureau's information: The Credit Agency, their address, their phone number, and the date the report was inquired or requested by you. There is also a number that represent any claims that you would make if the information need to be challenged

The next section is the your personal information. This includes the your name, social security number, up to three different addresses, date of birth (if available), and telephone number (if available).

Name: John Doe Consumer On File Since: 10/1/2002
SSN: ???-??-????
Address: Reported On: 5/1/2019
111 N LAKE Street Phone: 555-6439
ALTADENA CA 91104
Date of Birth: 04/19/2007

This next section of the report is employment information. This includes the company name, date hired (if available), income (if available), occupation (if available), and separation date (if available).

Company Name: ACCURATE CREDIT BUREAU
Date Hired: 11/1/2007
Income: $24K
Occupation: Laborer
Separation Date: 01/01/18

Report Summary

Here is the overall summary of the credit history. This will tell you and the lender the total number of accounts that you have. Accounts that are still currently active or negative or too new to be rated, accounts that are past due or paid off, person(s) that have inquired upon the applicant's credit history, accounts that are in collections or public records, total amount still owed, and a breakdown of the amount.

Your Report

Overall Summary

Total # of Trades: 14
Current Trades: 8
Unrated Trades: 1
Current Negative Trades: 5
History Negative Trades: 3
No. of Accts Paid: 5
Current Past Due: 4
Amount Past Due: $5,442 - 30 Days: 0 - 60 Days: 0 - 90+
Inquiries: 3
Inquiries. Last 6 months: 1
Public Records: 0
Collections Item: 2
Oldest Trade: 3/1/1994 –
Accounts Balance: $102,748
Monthly Payment: $1,348
Credit Limit: $0
High Credit: $107,247
Total Real Est. BAL. $77,576
Total Rev. BAL.
Total Installment Bal. $16,246
Available %: 0

Below are some of the variables that make up your credit score. I cannot express how important this space is. Remember me talking about money management? Now, match these variables to the foundation of you managing your money.

Total number of accounts
Accounts that are 30 days past due
Total amount that is still owed
Accounts that is still currently active
Accounts that are 60 days past due
Total minimum amount due every month
Accounts that are too new to be rated
Accounts that are 90+ days past due
Most amounts that can be borrowed

Currently active accounts that have been past due
Total number of inquired upon this credit history
Most amounts that has been owed
Past accounts that have been past due
Total number of inquiries within the past 6 months
Total amount of mortgage loans
Accounts that have been paid off
Total number of accounts that are in public records
Total amount of revolving balances (credit cards)
Currently active accounts that are past due
Total number of accounts that are in collections
Total amount of installment balances (loans)
Total amount of the past due accounts
Oldest account
Available percentage of the credit limit

The score summary is founded above your credit and trade information and is the overall rating of your credit. Up to four factors are disclosed and are displayed, in order, based on their relative impact on the final score. Generally, scores exceeding 625 are considered by banks as worthy of loans.

The lowest scores are in the low 400's and the highest scores are close to 850 (Very few). Scores between 600 and 700 are common and considered very good. Most people will fall between 550 and 650 credit scores.

Scores below 575 are considered a risk, and usually warrant further documentation or higher security deposits. This is what I plan to show you how to develop and build your scores.

Your Report

Scorecard: XXXX
Score: 676

Reasons codes:

1. Serious delinquency public record or collection filed
2. Level of delinquency on accounts
3. Time since delinquency is too recent or unknown
4. Proportion of balances to credit limits is too high on bank revolving or other revolving accounts

Please always focus on the Reason Codes when you do not know what to do. These codes reveal to you so much insight for your purpose to improve your score.

The next area is collections, it Identifies accounts that have been transferred to a professional debt-collecting firm. Collection information includes the name of the collection agency providing the information, collector's kind-of-business designators, and your account number with the collection agency.

Also included is the date the amount was charged off by the original creditor, date the information was verified, the original dollar amount of collection, the balance owed as of date verified or closed, name of the original creditor, and an explanation of current account status as reported by the collection agency.

Collection services
(9B) Collection account
Placed for collection 9/1/2001 7/1/2003
01Z5P001/MEDCLR IN 9037 139- $123
Collection services (9B) Collection account
Placed for collection 5/1/2003 6/1/2003
04326001/CRD PRT ASSO 889327752 -$96 $96

Collection services
(9P) Payment after charge off/collection
Paid collection 7/1/2002 1/1/2003 04326001/
CRD PRT ASSO 728157819 1/1/2003 $53 $0 Paid in full

PUBLIC RECORDS

7. If there are any civil actions with dollar amounts awarded, they will appear below the score summary in a field titled Public Records. Public Records information consists of bankruptcies, liens, and civil actions against you.

This information will include; the reporting account's name and number, original filing date with court, status date if status is satisfied, released, vacated, discharged or dismissed, amount and type of public record, certificate or docket number, and code describing your association to the public record. Also provided are the plaintiff name; liability and asset amount (for bankruptcies only), voluntary indicator (for bankruptcies only).

Chapter 7 bankruptcy discharged Federal District 99\05
Miscellaneous and public record 7/1/2003 11/1/2006
Individual account 05079095

Civil Judgment 99M1703591
Miscellaneous and public record 2/1/2007
Individual account 05027325

DOE JOHN X $1,975

Paid Civil Judgment Municipal Court 2C02730
Miscellaneous public record 10/1/2002 3/1/2008
Individual account 0508720V
JANE DOE $3,300

Your Report

Trade Lines

8. Under the trade lines portion of the credit report, creditors report the amount of loans and credit cards with payment histories. The name of the creditor is in the left column, the credit amount information in the center column, and the payment history is in the right column.

HHLD BANK/07991188 0293592399
Revolving account (09) Charged off as bad debt

Banks and S&Ls 400 $1,148 $0 $0 4/1/2000
Account was closed because of charge-off or repossession
Joint account

PEOPLES ENGY/026JX001
7500028283747
Open account
(9B)Collection account
Canceled by credit grantor 3/1/2002 4/1/2003

Utilities and fuel
$382 $382 $377 10/1/2002
Account was closed because of charge-off or repossession
Individual account

CAPITAL 1 BK/01DTV001
517805218329
Revolving account (05)120 days past due 4/1/2002

Banks and S&Ls $697 $739 $114 $22 9
554321111
MIN
Authorized account

Below are some of the variables that make up credit scores:

Name of the company
Date the account was opened
Most amounts the consumer can owe
Currently still owes
Minimum monthly payment
Number of times 30 days late
Number of times 60 days late
Number of times 90+ days late
Account number with the company
Date the account was last reported
Most amounts the consumer has owed
Amount that is past due
Number of months repaid
Payment pattern (Left being the most current)
Type of account
Kind of business of the company
Amount that was charged off
Original amount owed
Date the account was closed
Payment terms made with the company
Status of the account
Reason the account was closed
Users on the account
Notes about the account

Payment History

9. On the far right hand side of the report is the consumer payment history for the past 24 months. These codes reflect the monthly status of an account and are displayed for balance reporting loans. Collections and charge-offs are not graded.

These codes stand for:

0 Current account/zero balance-reported on update tape
1 Current
2 30 days past the due date
3 60 days past the due date
4 90 days past the due date
5 120 days past the due date
6 150 days past the due date
7 180 days past the due date
9 Collection
B Account condition change, payment code not applicable
X No history reported for that month

INQUIRIES

10. This portion of the report is named inquiries. This is a list of companies that have inquired about the applicant's credit, usually for the purpose of extending new or additional credit. Numerous inquiries lower the applicant's summary score by about two points per inquiry.

7/17/2003 NCO GRP 03899329
6/17/2003 FNB OF MARIN 02200488
4/23/2002 1ST PREMIER 00020123
3/13/2002 SURPAS CORP 00000001
1/10/2002 1ST PREMIER 00020123

Date the report was obtained, name of the company that inquired upon the report, company's subscriber number.

Warning Messages

11. The last portion of the report is called warning messages. This is a list of messages that relate to your credit, social security number, name, and address.

Credit data not suppressed

Current Address ALERT (house number mismatch): Mismatch - input does not match file

Surname ALERT: Mismatch - input does not match file

The first three messages mean that you have received all the products that were provided.

Address mismatch means the address provided by you is not on file with the credit bureaus. Surname mismatch means the last name used is not on file with the credit bureaus.

Credit Inquiries

A credit inquiry is an item on a credit report that shows a business with a "permissible purpose" (as defined under the federal Fair Credit Reporting Act) has previously requested a copy of the report.

Not all inquiries count toward your FICO score.

When you check your credit report, you may notice that a number of credit inquiries have been made, sometimes from businesses that you do not know. The only inquiries that count toward your score are the ones that result from your applications for new credit. Inquiries that count toward your FICO score.

Your Report

There is only one type of credit inquiry that counts toward your FICO score. When you apply for a mortgage, auto loan or other credit, you authorize the lender to request a copy of your credit report. These types of inquiries, prompted by your own actions, appear on your credit report and are included in your FICO score.

Inquiries that do not count toward your FICO score.
Your own credit report requests, credit checks made by businesses to offer you goods or services, or inquiries made by businesses with which you already have a credit account do not count toward your FICO score.

Credit checks by prospective employers also do not count. These types of inquiries may appear on your credit report, but they are not included in your FICO score. Your FICO score is not affected when you check your credit.

Checking your credit reports regularly to be sure they are accurate and error-free is a good idea. In fact, maintaining accurate credit reports is a part of good credit management, which can help to improve your FICO scores over time.

You can order more than one of your credit reports with FICO scores at myFICO.com. Checking your score at MyFICO does not count as an inquiry and will not hurt your FICO score.

Chapter Three

Scoring Model Facts

Most lenders make their decisions using FICO credit scores, which are based on five key factors. That means that when you apply for a new credit card or loan, these are the primary influences on whether you'll end up getting approved. Here are the five factors, in order of importance: payment history, credit utilization, length of credit history, credit mix and new credit inquiries.

35% – Payment history. Your ability to consistently make payments has the biggest impact on your score. Having late and missed payments is detrimental to your credit score, while a streak of on-time payments has a positive effect.

30% – Credit utilization. Your utilization measures how much of your available credit you're using across all of your cards. By using one-third or less of your total credit limit, you can help boost your score.

15% – Length of credit history. In general, having a longer credit history is helpful, though it depends on how responsibly you've used credit over time. Using credit well over time signals to lenders that you can be trusted to manage your finances.

10% – New credit. Applying for new credit leads to hard inquiries, which can negatively impact your credit score. Spacing out your new credit applications—and only applying for credit when you need it—helps your score.

10% – Credit mix. Having a variety of different types of credit—like credit cards, an auto loan or a mortgage—can influence your score as well. A diverse credit portfolio demonstrates your ability to successfully manage different types of credit.

With the knowledge of exactly how your score gets calculated, you can make smarter decisions with credit. Credit scores aren't as mysterious as they first appear, and you have control over all of the factors that determine your score. Money management is your ability to establish your score. Period!

These percentages are based on the importance of the five categories for the general population. For particular groups, such as people with relatively short credit histories, the importance of the categories may differ.

Inquiries are a subset of the "new credit" category shown above, which accounts for 10% of the total FICO score. Their importance depends on the overall information in your credit report.

For some people, a given factor may be more important than for someone else with a different credit history. In addition, as the information in your credit report changes, so does the importance of any factor in determining your score. What's important is the mix of information, which varies from person to person, and for any one person over time.

A FICO score takes into account only voluntary inquiries that result from your application for credit. The information about inquiries that can be factored into your FICO score includes:

- Number of recently opened accounts, and proportion of accounts that are recently opened, by type of account.
- Number of recent credit inquiries.
- Time since recent account opening(s), by type of account.
- Time since credit inquiry (ies).

For many people, one additional credit inquiry (voluntary and initiated by an application for credit) may not affect their FICO score at all. For others, one additional inquiry could take less than 5 points off their FICO score.

Inquiries can have a greater impact, however, if you have few accounts or a short credit history. Large numbers of inquiries also mean greater risk: People with six inquiries or more on their credit reports are eight times more likely to declare bankruptcy than people with no inquiries on their reports.

What happens when you apply for credit?

When you apply for credit, you authorize the lender to ask for a copy of your credit report. This is how voluntary inquiries appear on your credit report.

The inquiries section of your credit report contains a list of everyone who accessed your credit report within the last two years. The report you see lists both voluntary inquiries, spurred by your own requests for credit, and involuntary inquiries, such as when lenders order your credit report to offer you a pre-approved credit card.

Will your FICO score drop if you apply for new credit?

If it does, it probably will not drop much. If you apply for several credit cards within a short period, multiple inquiries will appear on your report.

Looking for new credit can equate with higher risk, but most credit scores are not affected by multiple inquiries from auto or mortgage lenders within a short period. Typically, these are treated as a single inquiry and will have little impact on the credit score.

What to know about "rate shopping."

Looking for a mortgage or an auto loan may cause multiple lenders to request your credit report, even though you are only looking for one loan. To compensate for this, the score ignores all mortgage and auto inquiries made in the 30 days prior to scoring. So if you find a loan within 30 days, the inquiries will not affect your score while you are rate shopping.

In addition, the score looks on your credit report for auto or mortgage inquiries older than 30 days. If it finds some, it counts all those inquiries that fall in a typical shopping period as just one inquiry when determining your score.

For FICO scores calculated from older versions of the scoring formula, this shopping period is any 14-day span. For FICO scores calculated from the newest versions of the scoring formula, this shopping period is any 45-day span.

Each lender chooses which version of the FICO scoring formula it wants the credit-reporting agency to use to calculate your FICO score.

Improving your FICO score.

If you need a loan, do your rate shopping within a focused period, such as 30 days. FICO scores distinguish between a search for a single loan and a search for many new credit lines, in part by the length of time over which inquiries occur.

Generally, people with high FICO scores consistently:

- Pay bills on time.
- Keep balances low on credit cards and other revolving credit products.
- Apply for and open new credit accounts only as needed.

Also, here are some good credit management practices that can help to raise your FICO score over time. These are basic practices and should become a way of management by you.

- Re-establish your credit history if you have had problems. Opening new accounts responsibly and paying them on time will raise your FICO score over the long term.
- Check your own credit reports regularly, and before applying for new credit, to be sure they are accurate and up-to-date. As long as you order your credit reports through an organization authorized to provide credit reports to consumers, such as MyFICO®, your own inquiries will not affect your FICO score.

The Credit Scoring Model

What it is...

The scoring system is licensed out to The Big Three credit repositories, which in turn call it by individual names to help differentiate which repository is issuing which score. Experian calls their score a FICO; Equifax calls theirs the Enhanced Beacon; and Transunion calls theirs the Empirica Model.

The score that each repository issues on their individual reports is a reflection of the information that repository has on an individual in their respective credit files. So, the score issued by each repository will usually be different from the other repository's scores.

The primary repository will usually have the most accurate score, and if the borrower has had any credit problems over the past few years, the primary repository will usually have the lowest credit score.

However, it will sometime work in reverse - if the borrower has recently cleaned up his credit history, the primary repository will usually have the most accurate updates, and in that case, the primary repository may likely show the highest score.

You can look at two different repository's reports on a borrower, and in reviewing the credit profiles; you can see what differences in the credit information are causing the different scores.

How It Works

Using a complex matrix measuring over 30 different variables in an individual's credit profile, the Fair, Isaacs program converts the profile into a numeric score, which is added to an individual's credit report.

That score is a reflection of the computer assigned credit risk for that individual. The intent is to reduce the amount of subjectivity credit decision makers (underwriters) inject into the risk analysis process.

The most important variables for mortgage loans are as follows:

Mortgage history
Derogatory Credit History
Liens or Judgments
Length of Credit History
Depth of Credit History
Proportion of Debt to Credit Balances
Amount of Available Credit

Generically speaking, the scores can run from 0 to 1,000. The highest I have ever seen is an 863. However, it is generally accepted that anyone with a 700 credit score is A credit, and over 720 is AA credit.

Individual lenders technically assign their own credit grades to the credit scores.

Score Model

Score Credit Grade

720 and up AA
700 to 719 A
680 to 699 A-/B+
660 to 679 B+/B
640 to 659 B
620 to 639 B-/C+/C
600 to 619 C/D
580 to 599 D/F
579 and below F

It is important to recognize that these scores are not just about derogatory credit history. They are about determining credit risk associated with a particular borrower, and points are added or taken away based on many different factors related to your credit profile.

For example, once you start using credit accounts, you are usually going to have a credit score in the 565 to 580 range. Why so low? Well, you are just starting out, and you have no credit history to rate.

Once you have 12 months of usage on your accounts, you will begin adding points to your credit history. However, if you mess up, you will destroy your credit quickly, and then you really face a tough uphill climb.

You are considered high risk when you start out, because you have not really proven yourself yet. As you slowly build credit over a year's time, your score will start climbing. Now the paradox sets in. Each time you add a new credit account to your history, your score will drop. Why?

Because you have added more debt to your credit load. However, once you have shown the ability to handle the new debt as well, your score will recover, usually in about six months. Once you have a 12-month rating on the new account, you will start having points added to your credit score. To score points, you have to use credit, and your creditors have to report your accounts to the credit bureaus.

You also have to pay your bills on time. Every time you show a late pay, you lose points, and it takes an awful long time to recover them. Once you show 36 months of timely payment history on any account, you are earning the maximum points.

Generally speaking, you will have an excellent credit score when you have four major accounts ($1,500 credit limits or higher) all with 36 months spotless payment history, and all usually maintaining balances that are at or below 60% of your available credit limits.

A mortgage rating will boost your score even further. You start collecting points on a mortgage at 12 months, and max out at 36 months.

Obviously, this too is where you will lose the most points if you have any late pays on your mortgage history is where it takes you the longest to recover any lost points.

Where you see scores in the 770 and up range, you will usually see about 8 to10 years history, with 3 to 4 revolving accounts that are rarely maxed out, a sterling mortgage history, and two or more major installment accounts (like car loans/leases) that have been paid off. If the report shows any late pays, it was likely a 30 day, one time, on a revolving account, over three years ago.

How about the person who never misses a payment, always pays on time, and still only has a 640 credit score? Well, if he uses a lot of credit, it could be that he has too many accounts, and he carries high balances (over 60%) in relation to the credit limits. Or he could be making too many minimum monthly payments, instead of sizable payments.

On the other hand, yesterday he had a 685 score, but today he has a new $25,000 credit card, with a new $20,000 balance on it. Alternatively, he has good credit, but he only has four accounts, no mortgage history, and three of the accounts are less than 24 months old.

The scoring model has weighted adjustments as well. The guy who has a strong credit history, and a lot of depth in his credit report, and blip... there pops up a 30 day late.

Well, it has been 60 days since, and the late pay was not on a mortgage or a car loan, so he is probably going to lose about 3 points on his credit score. If it was a mortgage or a car loan, he will lose about 10 points.

The guy with the 660 score? He is probably going to lose about 10 points on a revolving account late... if it is a mortgage or car loan, he might lose as much as 20 points. At 620, the revolving late will cost him 15 to 20 points, and a mortgage or car late could cost him a 30-point reduction in his score.

See, a computer cannot tell if you are a deadbeat, or under financial strain, or just nonchalant about paying your bills on time. Moreover, it really does not matter what the reason is.

All the computer knows is that if your score was already low, and you are making late payments, you are a credit risk - by giving you a low score, indicating you are a high credit risk, the credit report tells the next guy who loans you money that he is probably going to regret it!

Reliability of Scoring Models

For many people, it does not seem fair. Nevertheless, the truth is, with the advent of the scoring models, more people can borrow more money than ever before. Risk analysis has become more quantifiable, and lenders are more confident now with the predictability factors in their loan portfolio management.

Thus, they are comfortable offering more loan programs, and managing the risk by adjusting the interest rates and loan to value ratios according to credit score.

The models aren't perfect, and a lot of mistakes still occur. But there has been extensive research and verification on the reliability of the scoring models, by heavyweights such as FNMA and FHLMC.

The research holds up. If you are a 640 FICO, you are a greater risk than a 700 FICO individual is. You personally may never have a problem on a new loan, but of all the loans, that lender made to 640 FICO borrowers; he knows he is going to have a higher default rate that on the pool of loans he made to 700 FICO borrowers.

More than that, he knows approximately what the percentage rate difference of the defaults is going to be between the two groups, and he will adjust his interest rates to make up for the higher losses he is going to absorb for the lower scoring group.

He has no way of knowing if it will be you, or the other 640 FICO individuals who default... only that it will happen at a higher rate than 700 FICO defaults. In addition, of course, if you are a 600 FICO, the risk you pose more than doubles.

Now here is the fun part. Figuring out where you rate in terms of credit grade. For a car dealer, if you have two decent lines of credit, and you had a couple of payment problems over two years ago, but you have been clean since, even though your score is a 585, he's going to get you a loan.

To build you up, he tells you that you have "A" credit, so you are not paying as much attention to the financing being at 14.99% instead of the 8.99% that a real "A" borrower is getting. And not knowing any better, you go out the door thinking you are an "A" credit borrower.

Same thing with some of the consumer loan companies, or electronics stores, carpet stores, furniture stores and so forth that either carry their own financing, or have profit sharing arrangements with consumer finance companies.

It is worth keeping in mind that these types of companies can easily repossess the goods, or come after you in court, without a great deal of risk in terms of loss. It's a lot easier to get credit from those kinds of lenders.

Same things with credit card offers. But, these scores can make a big difference in the card offers you receive, what kind of credit limits they will ultimately give you, and what kind of interest rates they are going to charge - both introductory and long term.

If you have a 700 FICO score, everybody wants your business, and you are going to find your mailbox stuffed with credit card offers all the time. You are also going to see many 2.9% and 3.9% promotional rates for as long as 12-month periods, $10,000 to $25,000 credit lines, and long term fixed rates as low as 7.99%

If you are in the 660 to 699 range, you are mailbox is going to be stuffed too... and you will probably see a lot of six month 2.9% to 3.9% introductory offers as well. But you'll likely see most of your long-term rates hovering in the 12.99% to15.99% range.

Chances are, you will still see a lot of credit card offers in the 620 to 659 range, but you will be getting mostly generic standard high rate credit card offers.

Some will offer you 3.9% introductory rates, but most of them will be for about three months or so, and then the card rises up to 17.99% or higher, on a variable rate basis.

From 600 to 619, you will still get quite a few offers too, but not too many low introductory offers. You might even get one or two that might offer you up to a $5,000 credit limit, but most will be in the $1,000 to $3,000 range and you will be starting right out at the 17.99% and up variable rates.

With a 580 to 599 credit score, you will see a lot of offers too - but they will be for $500 to $1,000 credit lines, no introductory low rate offers, and most will be starting out in the 19.99% and up variable interest rate range.

Many of the offers will be for secured cards - in other words, to get the card, you have to post a savings account deposit with the card issuer, and you will only get a credit limit equal to your deposit. Most of these plans limit you to $500 until you show a 12-month rating on the account.

Chapter Four

The VantageScore

VantageScore is a credit scoring model that assigns you a score from 300 to 850 based on your credit health. What is your credit health? It is your money management and wealth creation goals in affect or the lack of a plan. Several factors, including payment history, credit usage and the age of credit accounts, affect an individual's VantageScore.

You can check your VantageScore for free to monitor your score over time, as well as track your progress as you work toward your financial goals.

While you may think of your credit score as a single number, the truth is that there isn't just one type of credit score — there are several. VantageScore is a credit scoring model created as a joint venture by the three major credit bureaus, Experian, Equifax and TransUnion. When you apply for credit, lenders may look up your VantageScore to help them decide whether to approve your application, and a higher VantageScore score may unlock more financial opportunities for you.

Here, we will discuss what VantageScore is, how the scoring model works and what factors influence the calculation of your VantageScore.

VantageScore vs. FICO

VantageScore and FICO are consumer credit scoring models that help lenders assess an applicant's creditworthiness. Both scoring models typically assign a score between 300 to 850 (though there are scoring variants with different ranges), with a higher score indicating stronger credit.

Although both VantageScore and FICO models take into account similar data, such as a your payment history, to generate credit scores, they use slightly different scoring models, meaning your VantageScore may differ from your FICO score.

VantageScore is calculated based on credit data pulled from all three credit reporting bureaus: Experian, TransUnion and Equifax. It takes into account several aspects of your credit history, then uses machine learning to predict your creditworthiness and assign you a score.

Here are the factors VantageScore utilizes when calculating your credit score include:

Payment history: How often you pay your bills on time, and whether there are missed or late payments in your credit history. A consistent payment history is one of the best ways to achieve good credit since it signals that you're more likely to repay your lenders.

Age and type of credit: The length of your oldest account and the types of credit you have access to. A longer credit history contributes to a good credit score, and a mix of credit — for example, an auto loan and a credit card — can potentially improve your score.

Credit utilization: The percentage of available credit that you're currently using. Lenders prefer low credit utilization, which signals that you're maintaining a manageable amount of credit. High credit utilization — for example, maxing out a credit card — can lower your score.

Total balance: The amount you still owe to lenders. A high balance often coincides with higher credit utilization, which can reduce your score.

Available credit: More available credit typically indicates a lower credit utilization ratio, which may increase your credit score.

Recent credit history: VantageScore considers recent hard inquiries into your credit history — for example, the credit check a lender may run when deciding whether to approve a credit application. Hard inquiries can have a small, temporary negative impact on your score.

Some factors are weighted heavier than others when determining a VantageScore, and the relative importance of each factor can vary between models.

VantageScore continually researches and develops new scoring methods, and its most recent scoring models are VantageScore 3.0 and VantageScore 4.0. Both models use a VantageScore range from 300 to 850, assigned based on an individual's credit history, as well as machine learning technology that predicts consumers' behavior.

As the latest scoring model, VantageScore 4.0 uses more advanced machine learning techniques than VantageScore 3.0. As a result, VantageScore 4.0 can assign more accurate scores to consumers with limited credit history, such as people new to the country who are building their credit in the United States. It also tracks changes in credit behavior over time, so consumers' recent credit behavior more accurately aligns with their score.

VantageScore ranges

VantageScores fall between 300 and 850, similar to FICO scores. A higher score indicates stronger credit, and achieving a good or excellent score may increase your chances of being approved for credit.

Lenders, including financial institutions, may look at your VantageScore when you apply for consumer credit, such as a new credit card, an auto loan, a personal loan or a mortgage. However, there are other situations where a third party may perform a credit check and look at your VantageScore.

For example, a potential landlord may look at your VantageScore when you apply to rent a home and telecommunications companies may run a credit check and view your VantageScore when you sign up for a new phone plan.

Part of monitoring your credit involves checking your credit history and your credit score from time to time. Fortunately, VantageScore allows consumers to request a free credit score.

To check your VantageScore, visit VantageScore's website, which lists providers that allow you to check your score for free. Log into your provider of choice to view your current VantageScore, and continue to re-check your score regularly — three to six times a year, depending on your goals — to track how it changes over time.

Achieving (or maintaining) a good or excellent VantageScore is a smart financial goal. Strong credit may not only make it easier to successfully apply for new credit when you need it, but also may help you secure more favorable interest rates than if you have a lower score.

Now that you understand which factors go into calculating your VantageScore, you can tailor your financial behavior to improve your credit. The following tips can help:

Make your payments on time, every time: A strong payment history significantly affects your VantageScore. Regularly paying your bills on time indicates creditworthiness, which can help raise your score.

Lower your credit utilization: A low credit utilization helps improve your credit score. Paying off your debts more aggressively — for example, by making more than the minimum monthly payment if your lender allows it — lowers your credit utilization and benefits your score.

Keep your oldest credit account open: A longer credit history can positively affect your credit. Your oldest account should remain open and in good standing to maximize your score.

Manage your credit applications: Several hard inquiries can temporarily lower your VantageScore. Ensure each new credit application fits into your financial strategy, and avoid excessive credit applications to minimize the impact on your score.

Finally, include checking your VantageScore, and your FICO score, as part of your ongoing credit monitoring plan. Keeping tabs on your VantageScore helps you track how your financial behavior affects your credit — for example, noticing a boost in your score after you pay off a credit card — and helps you stay motivated as you work toward your financial goals.

Chapter Five

The Average Credit Statistics & Facts

Here you are about to read the technical and actual facts about something that is in your total control. Everything about your financial life is in your hands.

You control your money, you will control your narrative, you control your narrative as you control your credit score. Remember your score affects your cost, your cost affects your wealth creation.

Number of Credit Obligations

On average, today's consumer has a total of 13 credit obligations on record at a credit bureau. These include credit cards (such as department store charge cards, gas cards, or bank cards) and installment loans (auto loans, mortgage loans, student loans, etc.).

Not included are savings and checking accounts (typically not reported to a credit bureau). Of these 13 credit obligations, 9 are likely to be credit cards and 4 are likely to be installment loans.

Past Payment Performance

On average, today's consumers are paying their bills on time. Less than half of all consumers have ever been reported as 30 or more days late on a payment. Only 3 out of 10 have ever been 60 or more days overdue on any credit obligation.

77% of all consumers have never had a loan or account that was 90+ days overdue, and less than 20% have ever had a loan or account closed by the lender due to default.

Credit Utilization

About 40% of credit card holders carry a balance of less than $1,000. About 15% are far less conservative in their use of credit cards and have total card balances in excess of $10,000.

When we look at the total of all credit obligations combined (except mortgage loans), 48% of consumers carry less than $5,000 of debt.

This includes all credit cards, lines of credit, and loans-everything but mortgages. Nearly 37% carry more than $10,000 of non-mortgage-related debt as reported to the credit bureaus.

Total Available Credit

The typical consumer has access to approximately $19,000 on all credit cards combined. More than half of all people with credit cards are using less than 30% of their total credit card limit. Just over 1 in 7 are using 80% or more of their credit card limit.

Length of Credit History

The average consumer's oldest obligation is 14 years old, indicating that he or she has been managing credit for some time.

In fact, found that 1 out of 4 consumers had credit histories of 20 years or longer. Only 1 in 20 consumers had credit histories shorter than 2 years.

Inquiries

When someone applies for a loan or a new credit card account - in short, any time one applies for credit and a lender requests a copy of the credit report - this request is noted as an “inquiry” in the applicant's credit file.

The average consumer has had only one inquiry on his or her accounts within the past year. Fewer than 6% had four or more inquiries resulting from a search for new credit.

Do any of your rates shopping within a few weeks.

If you are planning to buy a house or refinance, it pays to organize your efforts and request quotes from lenders in a short period of time. Credit score models are sophisticated enough to not count these as multiple inquiries.

Contact your lender if they reported your balance without a credit limit. It may be assumed as "maxed out" and negatively impact your score. Pay special attention to your "no pre-spending limit" cards that just report your balance and credit reporting companies typically will use the highest monthly balance as your credit limit.

Facts & Fallacies

Myth: My score determines whether or not I get credit.

Truth: Lenders use a number of facts to make credit decisions, including your score. Lenders look at information such as the amount of debt you can reasonably handle given your income, your employment history, and your credit history.

Based on their perception of this information, as well as their specific underwriting policies, lenders may extend credit to you although your score is low, or decline your request for credit although your score is high.

Myth: A poor score will haunt me forever.

Truth: Just the opposite is true. A score is a “snapshot” of your risk at a particular point in time. It changes as new information is added to your bank and credit bureau files. Scores change gradually as you change the way you handle credit.

For example, past credit problems impact your score less as time passes. Lenders request a current score when you submit a credit application, so they have the most recent information available. Therefore by taking the time to improve your score, you can qualify for more favorable interest rates.

Myth: Credit scoring is unfair to minorities.

Truth: Scoring considers only credit-related information. Factors like gender, race, nationality and marital status are not included. In fact, the Equal Credit Opportunity Act (ECOA) prohibits lenders from considering this type of information when issuing credit. Independent research has been done to make sure that credit scoring is not unfair to minorities or people with little credit history.

Scoring has proven to be an accurate and consistent measure of repayment for all people who have some credit history. In other words, at a given score, non-minority and minority applicants are equally likely to pay as agreed.

Myth: Credit scoring infringes on my privacy.

Truth: Credit scoring evaluates the same information lenders already look at - the credit bureau report, credit application and/or your bank file.

A score is simply a numeric summary of that information. Lenders using scoring sometimes ask for less information - fewer questions on the application form, for example.

Myth: My score will drop if I apply for new credit.

Truth: If it does, it probably won't drop much. If you apply for several credit cards within a short period of time, multiple requests for your credit report information (called “inquiries”) will appear on your report.

Looking for new credit can equate with higher risk, but most credit scores are not affected by multiple inquiries from auto or mortgage lenders within a short period of time. Typically, these are treated as a single inquiry and will have little impact on the credit score.

Negative credit items will eventually come off your credit report

Negative items on your credit report can cause damage to your credit score. Negative items include late payments, collection accounts, foreclosures and repossessions.

Although these items can lead to significant drops in your credit score, their effect is not permanent. Over time, negative items have a smaller and smaller impact on your score, as long as your credit behaviors improve so that more recent items are more favorable.

Additionally, most negative items should remain on your report for seven years at the most due to the regulations set by the Fair Credit Reporting Act. A bankruptcy, on the other hand, can last up to 10 years in some cases.

Bottom line: Negative items can cause a decrease in your credit score, but they aren’t permanent. Start building new credit behaviors and your score can recover over time.

The majority of lenders use FICO scores when making decisions

While there are multiple credit scoring models, the majority of lenders check FICO scores when making decisions. That means that when you apply for new credit—whether it's a credit card, a loan or a mortgage—the score that's more likely to matter is your FICO score.

That's important to know, because many free credit monitoring services will show you score estimates or your VantageScore. Some credit card companies provide a FICO score, however, and you can also request to see the credit score that lenders used to make their decision during the application process.

Fortunately, credit scoring models tend to reference the same data and weight factors fairly similarly. That means if you make on-time payments, keep your utilization low, avoid opening up too many new accounts and have a consistent credit history with a variety of accounts, you'll probably be in good shape regardless.

Bottom line: Knowing your FICO score can help you have an idea of how lenders will view your application for new credit.

You have many different types of credit scores

Credit scores vary based on the credit bureau reporting them and the credit scoring model used. The major credit bureaus all have slightly different information regarding your credit history. This means that these three, along with other credit reporting agencies, report several FICO credit scores to lenders to account for different information they've collected.

There are also different scores specific to particular industries. For example, auto lenders review different risk factors than mortgage lenders, so the scores each lender receives might differ. Although it can get confusing, the most important things to remember are the five core factors that affect your credit score.

Bottom line: Although many people reference their credit score in the singular, the truth is that there are many different types of credit scores that take into account different factors.

Checking your own credit won't hurt your score

Many people believe that checking their credit score or credit report hurts their credit, but fortunately, this isn't true. Getting a copy of your credit report or checking your score doesn't affect your credit score. These actions are called "soft" inquiries into your credit, and while they are noted on your credit report, they shouldn't have any effect on your score.

Checking your own credit score does not impact your credit at all

Hard inquiries, on the other hand, are noted when lenders look at your credit during an application process—and these can temporarily reduce your score. This is used to discourage you from applying for new credit too frequently. However, the effect is typically small, and after a couple of years the notation of a hard inquiry will leave your report.

Bottom line: You can check your own credit report and credit score without any negative effect—and we actually encourage you to do so to stay on top of your credit health.

You can check your credit score and credit reports for free

There are three main ways to check your credit for free. You'll likely want to take a look at both your credit reports and your credit scores. Here's how to get a hold of both of those:

You're entitled to a free credit report once each year by visiting AnnualCreditReport.com, a government-sponsored website that gives you access to your reports from TransUnion, Experian and Equifax.

You may be able to check your credit score free by contacting your bank or credit card company. Additionally, many free services— enable you to monitor your score for free. Just make sure to note which kind of credit score you're seeing, because there are many different scoring methods.

The information you find in your credit report lays out the factors that determine your credit score. By scanning your report closely, you'll likely find out the best strategy for improving your score—for instance, by improving your payment history or lowering your utilization.

Bottom line: Information about your credit is freely available, so take advantage of those resources to stay on top of your credit report and score.

Your credit score can cost you money

Ultimately, the purpose of credit scores is to help lenders determine whether they should offer you new credit, like a loan or a credit card. A lower score indicates that you may be at greater risk for default—which means the lender has to worry that you won't pay back your debts.

To offset this risk, lenders often deny credit applications for those with lower scores, or they extend credit with high interest rates. These interest rates can cost you a lot of money over time, so working to improve your credit score can have a measurable effect on your financial life.

Consider, for example, a $25,000 auto loan. With a fair credit score, you may secure an interest rate of 5.3 percent—so you'll pay a total of $3,513 in interest over five years. With an excellent credit score, your rate could drop to 3.1 percent, and you'll save nearly $1,500 in interest charges over that same five-year period.

Bottom line: A good credit score can have a positive impact on your finances, and a bad score can cost you money in interest charges.

Canceling old credit cards can lower your score

If you have a credit card that you're no longer using, you may be tempted to close the account entirely. Before doing that, though, consider how it could impact your credit score.

Recall that two credit factors are utilization and length of credit history. Closing an old account could affect one or both of those factors when it comes to calculating your score.

Your credit utilization could drop after closing an account because your credit limit will likely be lower. Since utilization represents all of your balances divided by your total credit limit, your utilization will go up if your credit limit goes down (and if your balances stay the same).

Your length of credit history could be lowered if you close an older account that is raising the average age of your credit.

Some people worry that having a zero balance on their credit card can negatively impact their score. This is just a credit myth. A zero balance means you aren't using the card to make any purchases.

Keeping the credit card open while not using it actually works to your benefit. You're able to contribute to the length of your credit history, while not risking the chance of debt and late payments.

You may need to use the card every now and then to avoid having it closed. Additionally, if the card has an annual fee, you may need to close the card or ask to have the card downgraded to a version that does not have a fee.

Still, if there's a way to keep the card open, it's often good to do so even if you don't plan to regularly use it. Bottom line: An old credit card can benefit your credit score even if you aren't using it anymore.

You can still get a loan with bad credit

It's true that getting a loan can be more difficult with bad credit, but it's not impossible. There are bad credit loans specifically for people with lower credit scores. Note, however, that these loans often come with higher interest rates—or they require some sort of collateral that the lender can use to secure the loan. That means if you don't pay your loan back, the lender will be able to seize the property you put up as collateral.

If you don't need a loan immediately, you could consider trying to rebuild your credit before applying. There are credit builder loans, which are specifically designed to help you build up a strong payment history and boost your credit score in the process. Unlike a traditional loan, you pay for a credit builder loan each month and then receive the sum after your final payment. Since these loans represent no risk to lenders, they're often willing to extend them to people with poor credit history looking to raise their score.

Bottom line: You can get a loan even with bad credit—but sometimes it's wise to find ways to raise your score before applying.

Credit scores aren't the only deciding factor for lending decisions

While credit scores are important in lending decisions, lenders may take other factors into account when deciding whether to offer you new credit. For example, your income and employment can play a significant role in your approval odds. Additionally, some loans (like auto loans and mortgages) are secured by collateral that the lender can seize if you default.

These loans may be considered less risky for the lender in certain cases because the asset can help offset any losses from nonpayment.

In many cases, your debt-to-income ratio is also an important factor in whether you're approved for a loan or credit card. Lenders consider your current monthly debt payments (from all sources) as well as your monthly income to determine whether you may be overextended financially.

Two different people may pay $1,500 each month for student loans, a car payment and a mortgage. That said, if one individual makes $3,500 each month and the other makes $8,000 each month, their situations will be considered very differently by a potential lender.

Bottom line: Keeping your credit score high can help you secure credit when you need it, but you'll want to stay on top of all aspects of your financial health.

Your credit report can help you spot fraud

Regularly checking your credit report can help you notice fraud or identity theft. If someone is using your information to open accounts, they will show up on your credit report.

If you notice an account that you did not open, you'll want to start taking steps to protect your identity from any further damage. You may also want to freeze or lock your credit, which prevents anyone from using your information to open up more accounts. Bottom line: Reviewing your credit report provides you an opportunity to notice when something is amiss.

Joint accounts affect your credit scores, but you do not have joint scores

If you have a joint account with someone else, that account will be reflected on both of your credit reports. For example, a loan that was opened by you and your spouse will show up for both of you—and will affect both of your credit scores. That said, your credit history, credit report and credit score remain separate. No one—including married couples—has a joint credit report or joint credit score.

In addition to joint accounts, you may also have authorized users on your credit card, or be an authorized user yourself. Authorized users have access to account funds, but they are not liable for debts. That means that if you make someone an authorized user on your credit card, they can rack up charges, but you'll be on the hook if they don't pay.

Because joint account owners and authorized users can influence credit scores in significant ways, we advise you to be careful about who you open accounts with or provide authorization to. Bottom line: Even though joint account owners and authorized users can influence someone else's credit, there are no shared credit reports or joint credit scores.

Many credit reports contain inaccurate credit information

The Federal Trade Commission found that one in five people has an error on at least one of their credit reports, and these inaccuracies can greatly impact your credit. This is why you should frequently check your credit report and dispute any inaccurate information. For example, since payment history accounts for 30 percent of your credit score, one wrong late payment can significantly hurt your score.

It's important to get your credit facts straight so you understand exactly how different things impact your score. One of the first things you should learn is how to read your credit report so you can quickly spot discrepancies and ensure that the information reported is fair and accurate.

After scrutinizing your credit report, you can look into other ways to fix your credit, like paying late or past-due accounts, so you can boost your score with your newfound knowledge. You can also take advantage of Lexington Law Firm's credit repair services to get extra help and additional legal knowledge to assist you.

As I am writing this book consumer credit reporting agency Equifax gave inaccurate scores to millions of Americans during a three-week period this year 2022. The Atlanta-based company — part of the "Big Three" of consumer credit reporting agencies that also includes Experian and TransUnion — allegedly provided the incorrect scores to those applying for home, car and credit card loans, according to the report, which cited "bank executives and others familiar with the errors."

In a statement, Equifax blamed the erroneous scores on a "coding issue" and said it has been fixed.

"Equifax identified a coding issue within a legacy, on-premise server environment in the U.S. slated to be migrated to the new Equifax Cloud™ infrastructure.

This issue, which was in place over a period of a few weeks, resulted in the potential miscalculation of certain attributes used in model calculations. Credit reports were not changed as a result of this issue," it said in part.

Bottom line: Your credit report could have inaccurate information that's hurting your score unfairly. Fortunately, there is a credit dispute process that can help you clean up your report and ensure all of the information on it is correct.

Chapter Six

Identity Theft

In the course of a busy day, you may write a check at the grocery store, charge tickets to a ball game, rent a car, mail your tax returns, change service providers for your cell phone, or apply for a credit card. Chances are you don't give these everyday transactions a second thought. But an identity thief does.

Identity theft is a serious crime. People whose identities have been stolen can spend months or years and thousands of dollars cleaning up the mess the thieves have made of a good name and credit record. In the meantime, victims of identity theft may lose job opportunities, be refused loans for education, housing, or cars, and even get arrested for crimes they didn't commit.

Humiliation, anger, and frustration are among the feelings victims experience as they navigate the process of rescuing their identity.

Working with other government agencies and organizations, the Federal Trade Commission (FTC) has produced this booklet to help you remedy the effects of an identity theft. It describes what steps to take, your legal rights, how to handle specific problems you may encounter on the way to clearing your name, and what to watch for in the future.

How Identity Theft Occurs

I first was notified that someone had used my Social Security number for his or her taxes in February 2004. I also found out that this person opened a checking account, cable and utility accounts, and a cell phone account in my name. I'm still trying to clear up everything and just received my income tax refund after waiting four to five months. Trying to work and get all this cleared up is very stressful.

Despite your best efforts to manage the flow of your personal information or to keep it to yourself, skilled identity thieves may use a variety of methods to gain access to your data.

How identity thieves get your personal information:
They get information from businesses or other institutions by:

1. Stealing records or information while on the job
2. Bribing an employee who has access to these records
3. Hacking these records
4. Conning information out of employees

- They may steal your mail, including bank and credit card statements, credit card offers, new checks, and tax information.
- They may rummage through your trash, the trash of businesses, or public trash dumps in a practice known as "dumpster diving."
- They may get your credit reports by abusing their employer's authorized access to them, or by posing

as a landlord, employer, or someone else who may have a legal right to access your report.

- They may steal your credit or debit card numbers by capturing the information in a data storage device in a practice known as "skimming." They may swipe your card for an actual purchase, or attach the device to an ATM machine where you may enter or swipe your card.
- They may steal your wallet or purse.
- They may complete a "change of address form" to divert your mail to another location.
- They may steal personal information they find in your home.
- They may steal personal information from you through email or phone by posing as legitimate companies and claiming that you have a problem with your account. This practice is known as "phishing" online, or pretexting by phone.
- How identity thieves use your personal information:
- They may call your credit card issuer to change the billing address on your credit card account. The imposter then runs up charges on your account. Because your bills are being sent to a different address, it may be some time before you realize there is a problem.
- They may open new credit card accounts in your name. When they use the credit cards and do not pay the bills, the delinquent accounts are reported on your credit report.

- They may establish phone or wireless service in your name.
- They may open a bank account in your name and write bad checks on that account.
- They may counterfeit checks or credit or debit cards, or authorize electronic transfers in your name, and drain your bank account.
- They may file for bankruptcy under your name to avoid paying debts they've incurred under your name, or to avoid eviction.
- They may buy a car by taking out an auto loan in your name.
- They may get identification such as a driver's license issued with their picture, in your name.
- They may get a job or file fraudulent tax returns in your name.
- They may give your name to the police during an arrest. If they do not show up for their court date, a warrant for arrest is issued in your name.
- If Your Personal Information Has Been Lost or Stolen
- If you have lost personal information or identification, or if it has been stolen from you, taking certain steps quickly can minimize the potential for identity theft.

Financial accounts: Close accounts, like credit cards and bank accounts, immediately. When you open new accounts, place passwords on them. Avoid using your mother's maiden name, your birth date, the last four digits of your Social Security number (SSN) or your phone number, or a series of consecutive numbers.

Social Security number: Call the toll-free fraud number of any of the three nationwide consumer reporting companies and place an initial fraud alert on your credit reports. An alert can help stop someone from opening new credit accounts in your name.

Driver's license/other government-issued identification: Contact the agency that issued the license or other identification document. Follow its procedures to cancel the document and to get a replacement. Ask the agency to flag your file so that no one else can get a license or any other identification document from them in your name.

Once you have taken these precautions, watch for signs that your information is being misused. If your information has been misused, file a report about the theft with the police, and file a complaint with the Federal Trade Commission, as well. If another crime was committed for example, if your purse or wallet was stolen or your house or car was broken into report it to the police immediately.

Identity Theft Victims: Immediate Steps

If you are a victim of identity theft, take the following four steps as soon as possible, and keep a record with the details of your conversations and copies of all correspondence.

1. Place a fraud alert on your credit reports, and review your credit reports.

Fraud alerts can help prevent an identity thief from opening any more accounts in your name. Contact the toll-free fraud number of any of the three consumer reporting companies below to place a fraud alert on your credit report.

You only need to contact one of the three companies to place an alert. The company you call is required to contact the other two, which will place an alert on their versions of your report, too.

Equifax: 1-800-525-6285; www.equifax.com; P.O. Box 740241, Atlanta, GA 30374- 0241

Experian: 1-888-EXPERIAN (397-3742); www.experian.com; P.O. Box 9532, Allen, TX 75013

TransUnion: 1-800-680-7289; www.transunion.com; Fraud Victim Assistance Division, P.O. Box 6790, Fullerton, CA 92834-6790

Once you place the fraud alert in your file, you're entitled to order free copies of your credit reports, and, if you ask, only the last four digits of your SSN will appear on your credit reports. Once you get your credit reports, review them carefully.

Look for inquiries from companies you haven't contacted, accounts you didn't open, and debts on your accounts that you can't explain. Check that information, like your SSN, address(es), name or initials, and employers are correct. If you find fraudulent or inaccurate information, get it removed.

Continue to check your credit reports periodically, especially for the first year after you discover the identity theft, to make sure no new fraudulent activity has occurred.

Fraud Alerts

There are two types of fraud alerts: an initial alert, and an extended alert.

- An initial alert stays on your credit report for at least 90 days. You may ask that an initial fraud alert be placed on your credit report if you suspect you have been, or are about to be, a victim of identity theft. An initial alert is appropriate if your wallet has been stolen or if you've been taken in by a "phishing" scam.

When you place an initial fraud alert on your credit report, you're entitled to one free credit report from each of the three nationwide consumer-reporting companies.

- An extended alert stays on your credit report for seven years. You can have an extended alert placed on your credit report if you've been a victim of identity theft and you provide the consumer reporting company with an "identity theft report."

When you place an extended alert on your credit report, you're entitled to two free credit reports within twelve months from each of the three nationwide consumer-reporting companies.

In addition, the consumer reporting companies will remove your name from marketing lists for pre-screened credit offers for five years unless you ask them to put your name back on the list before then.

To place either of these alerts on your credit report, or to have them removed, you will be required to provide appropriate proof of your identity: that may include your SSN, name, address and other personal information requested by the consumer reporting company.

When a business sees the alert on your credit report, they must verify your identity before issuing you credit. As part of this verification process, the business may try to contact you directly.

This may cause some delays if you're trying to obtain credit. To compensate for possible delays, you may wish to include a cell phone number, where you can be reached easily, in your alert. Remember to keep all contact information in your alert current.

2. Close the accounts that you know, or believe, have been tampered with or opened fraudulently.

Call and speak with someone in the security or fraud department of each company. Follow up in writing, and include copies (NOT originals) of supporting documents. It's important to notify credit card companies and banks in writing.

Send your letters by certified mail, return receipt requested, so you can document what the company received and when. Keep a file of your correspondence and enclosures.

When you open new accounts, use new Personal Identification Numbers (PINs) and passwords. Avoid using easily available information like your mother's maiden name, your birth date, the last four digits of your SSN or your phone number, or a series of consecutive numbers.

If the identity thief has made charges or debits on your accounts, or on fraudulently opened accounts, ask the company for the forms to dispute those transactions:

- For charges and debits on existing accounts, ask the representative to send you the company's fraud dispute forms. If the company doesn't have special forms, use the sample letter to dispute the fraudulent charges or debits. In either case, write to the company at the address given for "billing inquiries," NOT the address for sending your payments.

- For new unauthorized accounts, ask if the company accepts the ID Theft Affidavit. If not, ask the representative to send you the company's fraud dispute forms. If the company already has reported these accounts or debts on your credit report, dispute this fraudulent information.

Once you have resolved your identity theft dispute with the company, ask for a letter stating that the company has closed the disputed accounts and has discharged the fraudulent debts. This letter is your best proof if errors relating to this account reappear on your credit report or you are contacted again about the fraudulent debt.

Proving you is a Victim

Applications or other transaction records related to the theft of your identity may help you prove that you are a victim. For example, you may be able to show that the signature on an application is not yours. These documents also may contain information about the identity thief that is valuable to law enforcement.

By law, companies must give you a copy of the application or other business transaction records relating to your identity theft if you submit your request in writing. Be sure to ask the company representative where you should mail your request.

Companies must provide these records at no charge to you within 30 days of receipt of your request and your supporting documents.

You also may give permission to any law enforcement agency to get these records, or ask in your written request that a copy of these records be sent to a particular law enforcement officer.

The company can ask you for:

- Proof of your identity. This may be a photocopy of a government-issued ID card, the same type of information the identity thief used to open or access the account, or the type of information the company usually requests from applicants or customers, and

- A police report and a completed affidavit, which may be the Identity Theft Affidavit or the companies' own affidavit.

3. File a report with your local police or the police in the community where the identity theft took place.

Then, get a copy of the police report or at the very least, the number of the report. It can help you deal with creditors who need proof of the crime. If the police are reluctant to take your report, ask to file a "Miscellaneous Incidents" report, or try another jurisdiction, like your state police.

You also can check with your state Attorney General's office to find out if state law requires the police to take reports for identity theft. Check the Blue Pages of your telephone directory for the phone number or check www.naag.org for a list of state Attorneys General.

4. File a complaint with the Federal Trade Commission.

By sharing your identity theft complaint with the FTC, you will provide important information that can help law enforcement officials across the nation track down identity thieves and stop them.

The FTC can refer victims' complaints to other government agencies and companies for further action, as well as investigate companies for violations of laws the agency enforces.

You can file a complaint call the FTC's Identity Theft Hotline, toll-free: 1-877-IDTHEFT (438-4338).

Be sure to call the Hotline to update your complaint if you have any additional information or problems.

The Identity Theft Report

An identity theft report may have two parts:

Part One is a copy of a report filed with a local, state, or federal law enforcement agency, like your local police department, your State Attorney General, the FBI, the U.S. Secret Service, the FTC, and the U.S. Postal Inspection Service.

There is no federal law requiring a federal agency to take a report about identity theft; however, some state laws require local police departments to take reports. When you file a report, provide as much information as you can about the crime, including anything you know about the dates of the identity theft, the fraudulent accounts opened and the alleged identity thief.

Note: Knowingly submitting false information could subject you to criminal prosecution for perjury.

Part Two of an identity theft report depends on the policies of the consumer reporting company and the information provider (the business that sent the information to the consumer reporting company).

That is, they may ask you to provide information or documentation in addition to that included in the law enforcement report, which is reasonably intended to verify your identity theft.

They must make their request within 15 days of receiving your law enforcement report, or, if you already obtained an extended fraud alert on your credit report, the date you submit your request to the credit reporting company for information blocking.

The consumer reporting company and information provider then have 15 more days to work with you to make sure your identity theft report contains everything they need. They are entitled to take five days to review any information you give them.

For example, if you give them information 11 days after they request it, they do not have to make a final decision until 16 days after they asked you for that information. If you give them any information after the 15-day deadline, they can reject your identity theft report as incomplete; you will have to resubmit your identity theft report with the correct information.

You may find that most federal and state agencies, and some local police departments, offer only "automated" reports a report that does not require a face-to-face meeting with a law enforcement officer.

Automated reports may be submitted online, or by telephone or mail. If you have a choice, do not use an automated report. The reason? It's more difficult for the consumer reporting company or information provider to verify the information.

Unless you are asking a consumer reporting company to place an extended fraud alert on your credit report, you probably will have to provide additional information or documentation when you use an automated report.

Tips for Organizing Your Case

Accurate and complete records will help you to resolve your identity theft case more quickly.

- Have a plan when you contact a company. Don't assume that the person you talk to will give you all the information or help you need. Prepare a list of questions to ask the representative, as well as information about your identity theft.

Don't end the call until you're sure you understand everything you've been told. If you need more help, ask to speak to a supervisor.

- Write down the name of everyone you talk to, what he or she tells you, and the date the conversation occurred. Use Chart

Your Course of Action to help you.

- Follow up in writing with all contacts you've made on the phone or in person. Use certified mail, return receipt requested, so you can document what the company or organization received and when.
- Keep copies of all correspondence or forms you send.
- Keep the originals of supporting documents, like police reports and letters to and from creditors; send copies only.

- Set up a filing system for easy access to your paperwork.
- Keep old files even if you believe your case is closed. Once resolved, most cases stay resolved, but problems can crop up.

Investment Fraud

The SEC's Office of Investor Education and Assistance serves investors who complain to the SEC about investment fraud or the mishandling of their investments by securities professionals. If you believe that an identity thief has tampered with your securities investments or a brokerage account, immediately report it to your broker or account manager and to the SEC.

You can file a complaint with the SEC's Complaint Center at www.sec.gov/complaint.shtml. Include as much detail as possible. Write to the SEC at: SEC Office of Investor Education and Assistance, 450 Fifth Street, NW, Washington DC, 20549-0213. For answers to general questions, call 202-942-7040.

Mail Theft U.S. Postal Inspection Service (USPIS)

The USPIS is the law enforcement arm of the U.S. Postal Service, and investigates cases of identity theft. The USPIS has primary jurisdiction in all matters infringing on the integrity of the U.S. mail. If an identity thief has stolen your mail to get new credit cards, bank or credit card statements, pre-screened credit offers, or tax information, or has falsified change-of-address forms or obtained your personal information through a fraud conducted by mail, report it to your local postal inspector.

You can locate the USPIS district office nearest you by calling your local post office, checking the Blue Pages of your telephone directory.

Passport Fraud

If you've lost your passport, or believe it was stolen or is being used fraudulently, contact the USDS through their website, or call a local USDS field office. Local field offices are listed in the Blue Pages of your telephone directory.

Phone Fraud

If an identity thief has established phone service in your name, is making unauthorized calls that seem to come from and are billed to your cellular phone, or is using your calling card and PIN, contact your service provider immediately to cancel the account and/or calling card. Open new accounts and choose new PINs. If you're having trouble getting fraudulent phone charges removed from your account or getting an unauthorized account closed, contact the appropriate agency below.

- For local service, contact your state Public Utility Commission.
- For cellular phones and long distance, contact the Federal Communications Commission (FCC) at www.fcc.gov. You can file complaints online at www.fcc.gov, or e-mail your questions to fccinfo@fcc.gov.

Chapter Seven

Credit Repair Organizations

SEC. 401. SHORT TITLE.

This title may be cited as the 'Credit Repair Organizations Act'.

SEC. 402. FINDINGS AND PURPOSES.

(a) Findings.--The Congress makes the following findings:

(1) Consumers have a vital interest in establishing and maintaining their credit worthiness and credit standing in order to obtain and use credit. As a result, consumers who have experienced credit problems may seek assistance from credit repair organizations which offer to improve the credit standing of such consumers.

(2) Certain advertising and business practices of some companies engaged in the business of credit repair services have worked a financial hardship upon consumers, particularly those of limited economic means and who are inexperienced in credit matters.

(b) Purposes.--The purposes of this title are--

(1) to ensure that prospective buyers of the services of credit repair organizations are provided with the information necessary to make an informed decision regarding the purchase of such services; and

(2) to protect the public from unfair or deceptive advertising and business practices by credit repair organizations.

SEC. 403. DEFINITIONS.

For purposes of this title, the following definitions apply:

(1) Consumer. -- The term 'consumer' means an individual.

(2) Consumer credit transaction. -- The term 'consumer credit transaction' means any transaction in which credit is offered or extended to an individual for personal, family, or household purposes.

(3) Credit repair organization. -- The term 'credit repair organization'--

(A) Means any person who uses any instrumentality of interstate commerce or the mails to sell, provide, or perform (or represent that such person can or will sell, provide, or perform) any service, in return for the payment of money or other valuable consideration, for the express or implied purpose of--

(i) Improving any consumer's credit record, credit history, or credit rating; or

(ii) Providing advice or assistance to any consumer with regard to any activity or service described in clause (i); and

(B) Does not include--

(i) Any nonprofit organization which is exempt from taxation under section 501(c)(3) of the Internal Revenue Code of 1986;

(ii) Any creditor (as defined in section 103 of the Truth in Lending Act), with respect to any consumer, to the extent the creditor is assisting the consumer to restructure any debt owed by the consumer to the creditor; or

(iii) Any depository institution (as that term is defined in section 3 of the Federal Deposit Insurance Act) or any Federal or State credit union (as those terms are defined in section 101 of the Federal Credit Union Act), or any affiliate or subsidiary of such a depository institution or credit union.

(4) Credit.--The term 'credit' has the meaning given to such term in section 103(e) of this Act.

SEC. 404. PROHIBITED PRACTICES.

(a) In General.--No person may--

(1) make any statement, or counsel or advise any consumer to make any statement, which is untrue or misleading (or which, upon the exercise of reasonable care, should be known by the credit repair organization, officer, employee, agent, or other person to be untrue or misleading) with respect to any consumer's credit worthiness, credit standing, or credit capacity to--

(A) Any consumer reporting agency (as defined in section 603(f) of this Act); or

(B) Any person--

(i) Who has extended credit to the consumer; or

(ii) To whom the consumer has applied or is applying for an extension of credit;

(2) Make any statement, or counsel or advise any consumer to make any statement, the intended effect of which is to alter the consumer's identification to prevent the display of the

consumer's credit record, history, or rating for the purpose of concealing adverse information that is accurate and not obsolete to--

(A) Any consumer-reporting agency;

(B) Any person--

(i) Who has extended credit to the consumer; or

(ii) To whom the consumer has applied or is applying for an extension of credit;

(3) Make or use any untrue or misleading representation of the services of the credit repair organization; or

(4) Engage, directly or indirectly, in any act, practice, or course of business that constitutes or results in the commission of, or an attempt to commit, a fraud or deception on any person in connection with the offer or sale of the services of the credit repair organization.

(b) Payment in Advance.--No credit repair organization may charge or receive any money or other valuable consideration for the performance of any service which the credit repair organization has agreed to perform for any consumer before such service is fully performed.

SEC. 405. DISCLOSURES.

(a) Disclosure Required.--Any credit repair organization shall provide any consumer with the following written statement before any contract or agreement between the consumer and the credit repair organization is executed:

'Consumer Credit File Rights under State and Federal Law

You have a right to dispute inaccurate information in your credit report by contacting the credit bureau directly. However, neither you nor any "credit repair" company or credit repair organization has the right to have accurate, current, and verifiable information removed from your credit report.

The credit bureau must remove accurate, negative information from your report only if it is over 7 years old. Bankruptcy information can be reported for 10 years.

You have a right to obtain a copy of your credit report from a credit bureau. You may be charged a reasonable fee. There is no fee, however, if you have been turned down for credit, employment, insurance, or a rental dwelling because of information in your credit report within the preceding 60 days. The credit bureau must provide someone to help you interpret the information in your credit file.

You are entitled to receive a free copy of your credit report if you are unemployed and intend to apply for employment in the next 60 days, if you are a recipient of public welfare assistance, or if you have reason to believe that there is inaccurate information in your credit report due to fraud.

You have a right to sue a credit repair organization that violates the Credit Repair Organization Act. This law prohibits deceptive practices by credit repair organizations.

You have the right to cancel your contract with any credit repair organization for any reason within 3 business days from the date you signed it.

Credit bureaus are required to follow reasonable procedures to ensure that the information they report is accurate. However, mistakes may occur.

You may, on your own, notify a credit bureau in writing that you dispute the accuracy of information in your credit file. The credit bureau must then reinvestigate and modify or remove inaccurate or incomplete information.

The credit bureau may not charge any fee for this service. Any pertinent information and copies of all documents you have concerning an error should be given to the credit bureau.

If the credit bureau's reinvestigation does not resolve the dispute to your satisfaction, you may send a brief statement to the credit bureau, to be kept in your file, explaining why you think the record is inaccurate. The credit bureau must include a summary of your statement about disputed information with any report it issues about you.

(b) Separate Statement Requirement.--The written statement required under this section shall be provided as a document which is separate from any written contract or other agreement between the credit repair organization and the consumer or any other written material provided to the consumer.

(c) Retention of Compliance Records.--

(1) In general.--The credit repair organization shall maintain a copy of the statement signed by the consumer acknowledging receipt of the statement.

(2) Maintenance for 2 years.--The copy of any consumer's statement shall be maintained in the organization's files for 2 years after the date on which the statement is signed by the consumer.

SEC. 406. CREDIT REPAIR CONTRACTS.

(a) Written Contracts Required.--No services may be provided by any credit repair organization for any consumer

(1) Unless a written and dated contract (for the purchase of such services) which meets the requirements of subsection (b) has been signed by the consumer; or

(2) Before the end of the 3-business-day period beginning on the date the contract is signed.

(b) Terms and Conditions of Contract.--No contract referred to in subsection (a) meets the requirements of this subsection unless such contract includes (in writing)--

(1) The terms and conditions of payment, including the total amount of all payments to be made by the consumer to the credit repair organization or to any other person;

(2) A full and detailed description of the services to be performed by the credit repair organization for the consumer, including—

(A) All guarantees of performance; and

(B) An estimate of--

(i) The date by which the performance of the services (to be performed by the credit repair organization or any other person) will be complete; or

(ii) The length of the period necessary to perform such services;

(3) The credit repair organization's name and principal business address; and

(4) A conspicuous statement in bold face type, in immediate proximity to the space reserved for the consumer's signature on the contract, which reads as follows: 'You may cancel this contract without penalty or obligation at any time before midnight of the 3rd business day after the date on which you signed the contract. See the attached notice of cancellation form for an explanation of this right.'

SEC. 407. RIGHT TO CANCEL CONTRACT.

(a) In General. -- Any consumer may cancel any contract with any credit repair organization without penalty or obligation by notifying the credit repair organization of the consumer's intention to do so at any time before midnight of the 3rd business day which begins after the date on which the contract or agreement between the consumer and the credit repair organization is executed or would, but for this subsection, become enforceable against the parties.

(b) Cancellation Form and Other Information. -- Each contract shall be accompanied by a form, in duplicate, which has the heading 'Notice of Cancellation' and contains in bold face type the following statement:

'You may cancel this contract, without any penalty or obligation, at any time before midnight of the 3rd day which begins after the date the contract is signed by you.

To cancel this contract, mail or deliver a signed, dated copy of this cancellation notice, or any other written notice to (name of credit repair organization) at (address of credit repair organization) before midnight on (date)

I hereby cancel this transaction,

(Date)

(Purchaser's signature).'.

(c) Consumer Copy of Contract Required.--Any consumer who enters into any contract with any credit repair organization shall be given, by the organization--

(1) A copy of the completed contract and the disclosure statement required under section 405; and

(2) A copy of any other document the credit repair organization requires the consumer to sign, at the time the contract or the other document is signed.

SEC. 408. NONCOMPLIANCE WITH THIS TITLE.

(a) Consumer Waivers Invalid.--Any waiver by any consumer of any protection provided by or any right of the consumer under this title--

(1) Shall be treated as void; and

(2) May not be enforced by any Federal or State court or any other person.

(b) Attempt To Obtain Waiver.--Any attempt by any person to obtain a waiver from any consumer of any protection provided by or any right of the consumer under this title shall be treated as a violation of this title.

(c) Contracts Not in Compliance.--Any contract for services which does not comply with the applicable provisions of this title--

(1) Shall be treated as void; and

(2) May not be enforced by any Federal or State court or any other person.

SEC. 409. CIVIL LIABILITY.

(a) Liability Established.--Any person who fails to comply with any provision of this title with respect to any other person shall be liable to such person in an amount equal to the sum of the amounts determined under each of the following paragraphs:

(1) Actual damages.--The greater of--

(A) The amount of any actual damage sustained by such person as a result of such failure; or

(B) Any amount paid by the person to the credit repair organization.

(2) Punitive damages.--

(A) Individual actions.--In the case of any action by an individual, such additional amount as the court may allow.

(B) Class actions.--In the case of a class action, the sum of--

(i) The aggregate of the amount which the court may allow for each named plaintiff; and

(ii) the aggregate of the amount which the court may allow for each other class member, without regard to any minimum individual recovery.

(3) Attorneys' fees.--In the case of any successful action to enforce any liability under paragraph (1) or (2), the costs of the action, together with reasonable attorneys' fees.

(b) Factors to Be Considered in Awarding Punitive Damages.--In determining the amount of any liability of any credit repair organization under subsection (a)(2), the court shall consider, among other relevant factors--

(1) The frequency and persistence of noncompliance by the credit repair organization;

(2) The nature of the noncompliance;

(3) The extent to which such noncompliance was intentional; and

(4) In the case of any class action, the number of consumers adversely affected.

SEC. 410. ADMINISTRATIVE ENFORCEMENT.

(a) In General.--Compliance with the requirements imposed under this title with respect to credit repair organizations shall be enforced under the Federal Trade Commission Act by the Federal Trade Commission.

(b) Violations of This Title Treated as Violations of Federal Trade Commission Act.--

(1) In general. -- For the purpose of the exercise by the Federal Trade Commission of the Commission's functions and powers under the Federal Trade Commission Act, any violation of any requirement or prohibition imposed under this title with respect to credit repair organizations shall constitute an unfair or deceptive act or practice in commerce in violation of section 5(a) of the Federal Trade Commission Act.

(2) Enforcement authority under other law. -- All functions and powers of the Federal Trade Commission under the Federal Trade Commission Act shall be available to the Commission to enforce compliance with this title by any person subject to enforcement by the Federal Trade Commission pursuant to this subsection, including the power to enforce the provisions of this title in the same manner as if the violation had been a violation of any Federal Trade Commission trade regulation rule, without regard to whether the credit repair organization--

(A) Is engaged in commerce; or

(B) Meets any other jurisdictional tests in the Federal Trade Commission Act.

(c) State Action for Violations.--

(1) Authority of states. -- In addition to such other remedies as are provided under State law, whenever the chief law enforcement officer of a State, or an official or agency designated by a State, has reason to believe that any person has violated or is violating this title, the State--

(A) May bring an action to enjoin such violation;

(B) May bring an action on behalf of its residents to recover damages for which the person is liable to such residents under section 409 as a result of the violation; and

(C) In the case of any successful action under subparagraph (A) or (B), shall be awarded the costs of the action and reasonable attorney fees as determined by the court.

(2) Rights of commission.--

(A) Notice to commission.--The State shall serve prior written notice of any civil action under paragraph (1) upon the Federal Trade Commission and provide the Commission with a copy of its complaint, except in any case where such prior notice is not feasible, in which case the State shall serve such notice immediately upon instituting such action.

(B) Intervention.--The Commission shall have the right--

(i) To intervene in any action referred to in subparagraph (A);

(ii) Upon so intervening, to be heard on all matters arising in the action; and

(3) Investigatory powers. -- For purposes of bringing any action under this subsection, nothing in this subsection shall prevent the chief law enforcement officer, or an official or agency designated by a State, from exercising the powers conferred on the chief law enforcement officer or such official by the laws of such State to conduct investigations or to administer oaths or affirmations or to compel the attendance of witnesses or the production of documentary and other evidence.

(4) Limitation. -- Whenever the Federal Trade Commission has instituted a civil action for violation of this title, no State may, during the pendency of such action, bring an action under this section against any defendant named in the complaint of the Commission for any violation of this title that is alleged in that complaint.

SEC. 411. STATUTE OF LIMITATIONS.

Any action to enforce any liability under this title may be brought before the later of--

(1) The end of the 5-year period beginning on the date of the occurrence of the violation involved; or

(2) In any case in which any credit repair organization has materially and willfully misrepresented any information which--

(A) The credit repair organization is required, by any provision of this title, to disclose to any consumer; and

(B) Is material to the establishment of the credit repair organization's liability to the consumer under this title, the end of the 5-year period beginning on the date of the discovery by the consumer of the misrepresentation.

SEC. 412. RELATION TO STATE LAW.

This title shall not annul, alter, affect, or exempt any person subject to the provisions of this title from complying with any law of any State except to the extent that such law is inconsistent with any provision of this title, and then only to the extent of the inconsistency.

SEC. 413. EFFECTIVE DATE.

This title shall apply after the end of the 6-month period beginning on the date of the enactment of the Credit Repair Organizations Act, except with respect to contracts entered into by a credit repair organization before the end of such period.".

1. Pub. L. No. 104-208, 110 Stat. 3009 (Sept. 30, 1996). The amendments to the credit statutes are in Title II of the Act, entitled "Economic Growth and Regulatory Paperwork Reduction." The footnotes in this copy of the Act are not part of the Act, but are cross-references inserted by the FTC staff for the convenience of the reader.

2. Truth in Lending Act § 103(f) states in pertinent part: "The term 'creditor' refers only to creditors who regularly extend, or arrange for the extension of, credit which is payable by agreement in more than four installments or for which the payment of a finance charge is or may be required, whether in connection with loans, sales pf property or services, or otherwise. . . ."

3. TILA § 103(e) states: "The term 'credit' means the right granted by a creditor to a debtor to defer payment of debt or to incur debt and defer its payment."

4. Fair Credit Reporting Act (FCRA) § 603(f) states: "The term 'consumer reporting agency' means any person which, for monetary fees, dues, or on a cooperative nonprofit basis, regularly engages in whole or in part in the practice of assembling or evaluating consumer credit information or other information on consumers for the purpose of furnishing consumer reports to third parties, and which uses any means or facility of interstate commerce for the purpose of preparing or furnishing consumer reports."

Chapter Eight

Credit Repair

Your credit score is only as good as the information on your credit reports. When a credit report doesn't paint an accurate or complete picture of your credit history, that's when you need credit repair.

You can do it yourself. Credit report errors are extremely common. The more negative or misinformation you remove from your credit reports, the healthier your credit score can possibly become.

As I talk about credit repair please remember money management. Everything about your credit score is about your actions. Do not overthink this, people find themselves in a financial lockdown at times and their credit takes a few hits.

But there are times for which the three credit reporting agencies fail to get complete information and these errors begin to have a negative impact on your score. I want you above all things to start maintaining a strong, accurate credit report long term. Anything less is not acceptable.

Nor can you reduce this down to a single process of paying someone to do what you can do for yourself. If you are in the pursuit of wealth creation, then you understand the mindset required for you to accomplish that financial goal.

On the contrary, if you just want to get the car or credit card and are not too concerned with bringing wealth creation in your life at this time, then these final words may benefit you the most.

I am hopeful that you will continue to grow in knowledge and wisdom that you can reach your desired goals. It is all about you, keep it personal.

Credit Repair 101

Let's start at the beginning: What is credit repair? At a very basic level, credit repair is about cleaning up your credit report to boost your credit score. But you truly boost your score by the money management process that I talked about earlier.

Credit repair agencies try to help individuals improve their credit scores by reviewing their credit reports and correcting or removing negative or incorrect information that was bringing down the score.

This can be a double edge sword. Accurate information that is negative if challenged can cause the credit reporting companies to add a statement indicating that this negative information is being reported accurately, this can do harm.

Let's look at some examples of common credit report errors that happen from time to time. Credit repair companies look for accounts incorrectly reported to the credit bureaus as delinquent or late, closed accounts reported as open, accounts that falsely list an authorized user as an account owner, and accounts that don't actually belong to you.

I am constantly asked if credit repair costs money, if you do it on your own, it's free, but if you go through an agency, there are different levels of services, and fees are usually charged monthly.

As far as the exact costs go, I've seen crazy numbers ranging from less than $30 per month up to $100 per month or more. Credit repair agencies may try to sell you all kinds of things, but no matter what, they have to disclose the costs upfront.

This is where you need to be watchful, these agencies often do not inform you of the cost upfront or the actual services that they are offering you. Never be anxious about anything in this arena. If you give them your information you are trusting that whatever they do it will have a positive impact.

Please remember that if it's not positive then it ends up negative only on your personal financial fingerprint not theirs.

There is a process to Credit Repair and what credit repair companies do to get errors fixed or information taken off a consumer's credit report is something you can do yourself. Credit repair companies will submit disputes to the credit bureaus on your behalf. A dispute is simply a formal request to verify the accuracy of a piece of information on the credit report.

Credit bureaus have 30 days by law to respond to a dispute and during that time, the items being disputed aren't factored into your credit score. If they're unable to verify the disputed information on the report, they must fix or remove it entirely. It is really that simple.

Remember this is not something only those credit repair companies can do, as I said earlier most of that stuff you can do on your own. You can contact the credit bureaus and the creditors yourself. It's always a good idea to access credit reports from all three bureaus (Experian, Equifax, and TransUnion) to verify that information is consistent across the board.

If you find an error on one credit report, they'll likely be present on the other two, or not even reported there. It could be as simple as contacting the creditor to update the reporting, and if that doesn't work, then there is the option to send a dispute letter to the bureaus.

So is there anything you'd get by working with a credit repair company that you wouldn't get by fixing credit report errors on your own?

The thing that you get from working with a credit repair agency could certainly save you the time and frustration of trying to navigate the credit world yourself. They will also know what can and cannot be done with a credit report, whereas you may not even know where to begin.

Credit repair companies may also include legal action as part of the credit repair process if disputing information doesn't produce results. This can be in the form of a cease-and-desist letter to debt collectors on your behalf, but not every credit repair company will offer this and the process could vary by company and the individual's needs.

Be forewarned that any cease-and-desist letter to a debt collector can expedite action against you, not the credit repair company. Even though you have the right to issue such a letter, the law is clear stating that your creditor must cease immediately except to notify you of a lawsuit against you being filed.

It's not an overnight process. You should expect it to take three to six months to resolve most of the disputed debts. On the lower end, you could be looking at 30 days. If there are lots of issues, it could take over a year.

You should watch out for many things, every time I hear people tell me that somebody was guaranteeing something, I pause. That's a red flag. I've been in this industry for well over 20 years, and the one guarantee I can make is that there are no guarantees.

Sometimes promises to get rid of things on credit reports are not always realistic. There are a lot of factors that are beyond anybody's control. The credit repair agency still has to go to the credit bureaus and then to the creditors for resolution.

They cannot make the change themselves. Because of all the variables, they can't really promise a definitive timeline either, and if they do, that's concerning. If a company asks for money upfront, that's also a red flag to me.

It's no different, in some ways, to having your car fixed. You could open the hood of my car and be able to tell me that there's 10 things wrong with it, but I won't know what I'm looking at.

And I can only hope that I went to an honest and reliable mechanic who doesn't take advantage of that opportunity—people who don't really have an understanding of what's under the hood. It's the same thing in the credit world.

The language, the definitions, the lingo can be so foreign that it becomes challenging to know what you're looking for, especially when you get on the phone with a really good, fast-talking salesperson. They're going to sell you their service or product, so the key is to make sure that you work with a reliable agency.

Credit repair companies can offer services in most states, but not all. Before you pursue credit repair help, make sure it's legal where you live. This should make sense. Finding a reliable credit repair agency you have to do your research and ask questions.

Talk to other people who might've had experiences with those agencies, and then be your own advocate. Define what you are looking for. Say, "This is what I'm looking to do... Is that realistic, or am I not understanding the process well?" A good credit repair agency should be able to tell you what they can and cannot do for you upfront.

Under the Fair Credit Reporting Act you have the right to clean up your credit report so it is accurate.

1 And then there's something called the Credit Repair Organizations Act, which also regulates the credit repair industry.

2 It gives you the right to authorize somebody to make disputes on your behalf, but the main purpose of that Credit Repair Organizations Act is to set parameters to companies or organizations that offer credit repair services.

For example, a credit repair agency can't claim exactly how much their service would improve that score. They also can't alter somebody's identity, or charge advanced fees.

Know that there is a difference between credit counseling and credit repair. Those are two completely different ball games. Credit repair has to do with looking at the credit report, disputing errors and inaccuracies, or otherwise managing what's on the credit report.

Credit counseling is a service that educates you about things like budgeting and dealing with debt. Think of it like a broad coaching program that covers many different areas of personal finance. Credit repair simply focuses on the black and white of credit reports.

Credit Report Maintenance

What are some things you can do to keep your credit report in good shape without using a credit repair company, or after working with one?

The number one thing people should be doing is checking their credit reports at least once a year. Really take a good look at the type of debt, how much debt you have, and the debt-to-available-credit ratio [also called your credit utilization ratio] on your credit reports. See if there's old information that shouldn't be on there any more, or errors.

You're entitled to one free credit report from each of the three main credit bureaus each year from AnnualCreditReport.com.

You could also set up credit alerts. It's very important that you know who's checking your credit, and when, so you can spearhead anything that might be potentially fraudulent right when you get a notice. I think that's really important for keeping your credit score healthy.

If you make credit management part of your regular financial lifestyle, like budgeting, then you can manage issues when they pop up and you might not need somebody to fix a bigger issue later.

For a moment or a lifetime!

There is a story here that really represents the reality of credit repair. You can drink the gallon of water now and fulfill your amazing dreams that you desire right now.

Or, you can take the water and do the hard work of managing your money, being intentional with your action and use the water to prime the well and receive an abundance of what you may ever desire.

Think About It!

Chapter Nine

Final Words...

Wealth creation begins with every single step that you make. I just talk about credit repair because I already know that the majority of you wants it fast and now. But those of you who want it as a permanent part of your financial life please listen carefully.

I know that having a credit score that will enhance your ability to secure loans is always seen as a hard task. The fact that it seems hard keeps your minds away from even investing intentionally on having a high credit score. Please let this sink in and think closely about how it relates to you.

When the level of your credit score makes it easy for you to stand a chance of getting car loans with ease and keeps you in the position of paying at your convenient time frame with low interest the world seems great. Having a good credit score also gives you the benefit of getting more loans, and when loans are remitted on time and accurately it makes you benefit more.

One of the outstanding and mind thrilling reasons why you should get involved in making your credit score increase is because this has a great impact on your ability to continue wealth creation. Repeated moves to secure loans and paying up appropriately has made you beneficiaries of getting your personal and companies or organization stocked with needed items, getting land properties or getting it built in a short while, and making other rapid successes in your life's pursuit.

This should not be seen as a goal that cannot be attained or achieved, it is something that can be brought into your reality easily if you go through the right processes of money management.

If you want to have a personal car; you can get a loan today, if you want a new car because the old one is outdated, you can also get a loan and benefit from it today. It does not mean that you are where you should be financially.

It can be difficult for you to just stop and shift your behavior. That is why I highly recommend all of my other books. Money management is the key to great credit scores. Most people do not want to hear this but it is so true. There are companies that even offer alternative credit, credit scores and everything in between.

You should ask yourself, do I want to take shortcuts to try and improve my financial life? Think about all of the processes that are required to try to increase your credit score. Everything about it is from a negative aspect or the language just sounds a bit tricky. Let go through that approach if you have never heard of it, which I doubt.

Listen any time you apply for some form of credit or a loan, someone is checking your credit report. And if you have a low credit score, they say it's game over. You won't get approved or maybe with a high rate. Here comes the pitch.

The good news is you CAN increase your credit score - plus it's not hard, and it won't cost you a fortune. We can help people fix their credit. We help people achieve their financial goals that allow them to live the life they've always wanted, and to live the life they deserve. (By disputing not building credit.)

So listen carefully, because I'm going to tell you EXACTLY what to do to raise your credit in the quickest, most efficient and affordable way possible.

Do you know that removing negative items is the fastest way to raise your credit score? The two most common negative items on your credit report that hurts your score are collections and inquiries. I hope you are following me, oh I know that you are, this is what you want.

First let's talk about inquiries. These are what show up on your credit report every time you apply for credit. Inquiries will remain on your credit report for up to 2 years, and can lower your score by 3-7 points per inquiry. (Not True)

Plus, if you have too many inquiries on your credit report within the last 6 months (like more than 5-6), this alone could get you denied for loans, credit cards, mortgages, etc. (True)

Now onto collections. These show up on your credit report once you've failed to make payments on an account for more than 6 months. Once you've stopped paying, the creditor notifies the credit bureaus and sells your debt to a debt collector. (Not true) Not only do collections drastically lower your credit score, but even a single collection could stop you from getting approved for credit. (True)

I paused for a second here, what did you really just learn here? Money management that allows you to control your borrowing needs and paying your bills on time will manage your inquiries and collections. I am just saying, if you listen to the spill that credit repair people give you it says a lot.

This is where they provide fear to those of you who don't know better. Every inquiry on your credit report can lower your score by up to 3-7 points, which can add up fast. For example, if you have 5 to 10 inquiries on your report right now - you could be losing out on 35 to 70 points from your credit score.

Collections are even worse. A single collection could lower your score by up to 50 to 100 points, and if you have multiple collections then you could be losing out on HUNDREDS of points from your credit score.

Then you want a bit of personal security and ask is it really possible to remove these negative items?

YES! A little known fact is that many companies perform a credit inquiry on your report without having proper consent. If this is the case, then they are violating a federal law called the Fair Credit Reporting Act (FCRA). I talked about facts about inquiries earlier, (proper consent) that statement is practically true, but soft inquiries (promotional inquiries) there are no loss of points.

Debt collectors are also bound by the FCRA, as well as the FDCPA (Fair Debt Collection Practices Act). They must be able to provide proof that you owe the debt, they must be legally allowed to collect the debt, they must be licensed to collect in your state, and the list goes on. But who makes sure they are following the law? You do! (Again the facts are being manipulated)

As a consumer, you have the legal right to dispute the validity of any collection, inquiry, or account on your credit report. Upon doing so, the debt collector or the company who performed an inquiry must provide documented proof that they have followed all applicable laws and regulations.

If they fail to provide this proof, then the credit bureaus are required to remove the negative items from your credit report - thus raising your credit score. (This is true) But are you really hearing what I am saying? Are you?

You're probably wondering if this is a difficult and time consuming process -- it is, if you try and do it all by yourself. But that's where credit repair people come in and make claims of making your life a lot easier.

Trust me when I tell you that there are NOT any tricks to making this STUFF work. When you begin to seek after wealth creation and apply the value system to your process you will see this magical credit repair for what it is. Here is the hard final pitch.

The Closing

Anyone can open a dispute online with their credit bureaus, and it almost never works. The online system is designed to work against you. It's not surprising, because credit bureaus are in the business of putting information ON your credit report, not taking things OFF your credit report.

If you see any questionable information on your credit report (such as potentially inaccurate or erroneous collections or inquiries), the trick is to send a physical letter demanding proof and challenging the legality of the collections and inquiries in question. If they fail to provide adequate proof within 30 days, the credit bureaus must remove those negative items from your credit report.

My final words with this for now are the following. The fact that you are reading this, tells me that you are searching for something better. If you made it this far, I believe that you want something different. Wealth creation becomes a life skill that you are in pursuit of everyday.

You have the ability to see the good as well as the bad is one of the most important of all life skills. We all know there is a great deal of bad out here in the financial arena, but there is a great deal of good as well.

Many people let the bad things in life overwhelm them, and they are therefore unable to see past that bad to all the good things in life.

One reason the bad in life can seem so overwhelming is the fact that so much of it draws you in with fast pleasure. It takes you away from your real purpose. DELAY IS NOT DENIAL. Another reason for this focus on the bad is of course the fact it is often more interesting and intriguing than doing the right thing. For instance, while the building of your credit and money management may get scant attention, the likelihood of credit repair is likely to get your attention.

I know focusing on the alternative is perhaps an unavoidable part of human nature, but it is important to fight that impulse as much as possible. Focusing too much on the alternative in life can lead to a number of negative side effects, including greater levels of stress and anxiety, increased health problems and decreased quality of life. Not to mention bad credit and scores with high interest rates.

There are a number of tactics people use to focus on the good in life and it is important to choose the approach that works best for you. Some of the many ways people attempt to banish the alternative include learning relaxation and meditation techniques, practicing yoga and following a healthy diet. In addition, exercise itself can often lift your spirits and help you escape from those unwanted aspects of your life.

There are many wealth creation benefits to money management. So many people see the glass half full, as they say, often enjoy a greater level of financial freedom than those who choose to see that proverbial half empty glass.

The Closing

I do not have to tell you that there are many studies that show that pessimists have a great many more problems than optimists, so it does make good sense to see your financial life in a positive light. While it can sometimes be difficult to keep your chin up in such a strange environment, it is important to try to create the good in wealth creation.

Thank you greatly for giving ear to thoughts.